Inktober
2023

By
3ichael 7ambert

Michael Andrew Lambert Jr

Inktober is..

Inktober is an annual artistic challenge that invites creators from around the world to embrace the timeless beauty of ink. Originating in 2009, artist Jake Parker introduced this month-long event as a way to cultivate positive habits, improve drawing skills, and foster a global community of artists.

Throughout the month of October, participants, fondly known as "Inktoberists," embark on a creative journey by producing one ink-based artwork each day, guided by a set of daily prompts. These prompts are intentionally broad, allowing for a diverse range of interpretations and artistic styles.

Inktober not only serves as a platform for artists to showcase their talents but also fosters a sense of camaraderie within the creative community. Social media platforms come alive with a vibrant display of inked illustrations, providing a visual feast for art enthusiasts and aspiring creators alike.

Whether you are an established artist or a budding talent, Inktober stands as a testament to the power of daily artistic practice, the joy of experimentation, and the boundless possibilities that emerge when imagination meets ink.

So, dive into the enchanting world of ink, and let your creativity flow freely during this annual celebration of artistic expression.

Inktober List

DAY I	DREAM
DAY II	SPIDERS
DAY III	PATH
DAY IV	DODGE
DAY V	MAP
DAY VI	GOLDEN
DAY VII	DRIP
DAY VIII	TOAD
DAY IX	BOUNCE
DAY X	FORTUNE
DAY XI	WANDER
DAY XII	SPICEY
DAY XIII	RISE
DAY XIV	CASTLE
DAY XV	DAGGER
DAY XVI	ANGEL
DAY XVII	DEMON
DAY XVIII	SADDLE
DAY XIX	PLUMP
DAY XX	FROST
DAY XXI	CHAINS
DAY XXII	SCRATCHY
DAY XXIII	CELESTIAL
DAY XXIV	SHALLOW
DAY XXV	DANGEROUS
DAY XXVI	REMOVE
DAY XXVII	BEAST
DAY XXVIII	SPARKLE
DAY XXIX	MASSIVE
DAY XXX	RUSH
DAY XXXI	FIRE

In the realm of artistic expression, the choice of medium becomes a deeply personal decision, shaping the very essence of the creative journey. For this collection, I deliberately opted for the humble ballpoint pen—a seemingly mundane tool with an extraordinary capacity for nuance and subtlety.

The ballpoint pen, often overlooked in the realm of traditional art, becomes my steadfast companion throughout this Inktober odyssey. Its indomitable ink flow dances across the pages, unfurling a tapestry of lines and shades that bear witness to moments of inspiration and introspection.

While some may argue that ballpoint pens lack the finesse of other art supplies, it is precisely their inherent imperfections that drew me in. Each stroke tells a story of resilience, embracing smudges and uneven lines as the fingerprints of a creative journey. In the pages that follow, you'll encounter a spectrum of outcomes—some may not boast technical perfection, but within each stroke lies a genuine expression of artistic vulnerability.

Within these inked pages, I invite you to explore the dichotomy of the imperfect and the proud. As I present this collection, I find pride not only in the meticulously crafted pieces but also in the moments where the pen danced freely, leaving behind traces of raw, unfiltered creativity.

So, let us celebrate the unpredictable beauty of ballpoint pen art —a medium that whispers tales of daring exploration, steadfast dedication, and the unapologetic embrace of imperfection.

- Michael A. Lambert Jr

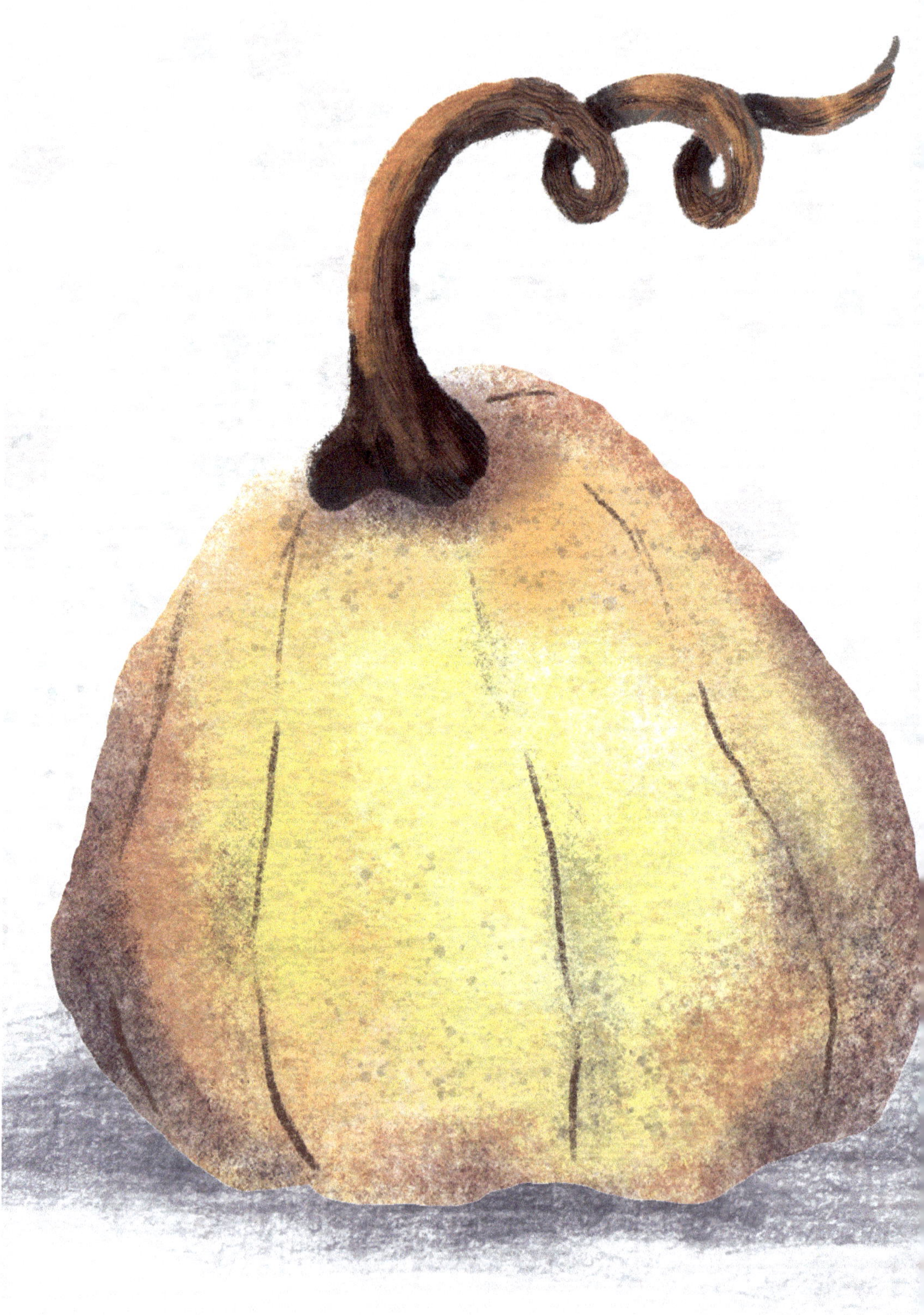

DAY I
DREAM

Embarking on the enchanting journey of transforming ephemeral thoughts into tangible realms on paper, I dedicated my initial strides to the art of typography. Day 1 unfolded with aspirations and dreams taking center stage. Through the deliberate arrangement of letters, I breathed life into the words that encapsulated my aspirations, allowing the strokes and curves to echo the contours of my imagination. Each typographic expression became a nuanced brushstroke, capturing the essence of the dreams that sparked the inception of this creative odyssey. As the ink met the canvas, Day 1 marked the commencement of a visual narrative, where typography became the vessel for translating the ethereal into the palpable.

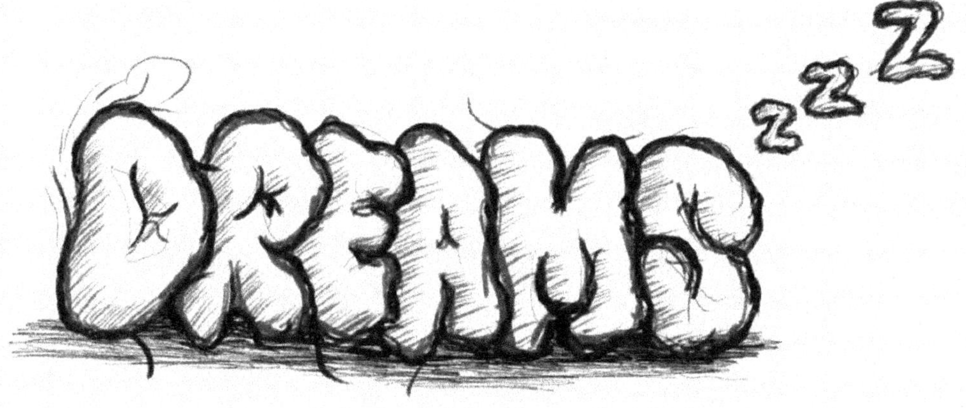

DAY II
SPIDERS

On Day II of this artistic expedition, the theme "SPIDERS" took center stage, leading me to wield the pen in an attempt to capture the essence of a black widow. Drawing solely from memory, the endeavor proved to be a humbling exercise as the intricate details eluded my pen, resulting in a portrayal that fell short of accuracy. Yet, within the imperfection lies a lesson—an acknowledgment of the challenges inherent in translating mental images onto paper. As the black widow emerged with its own unique character, this moment became a stepping stone, encouraging me to embrace the unexpected twists that creativity unfurls. Day II, marked by the discrepancy between mental imagery and artistic execution, served as a reminder that each stroke, whether precise or imperfect, contributes to the evolving narrative of this creative journey.

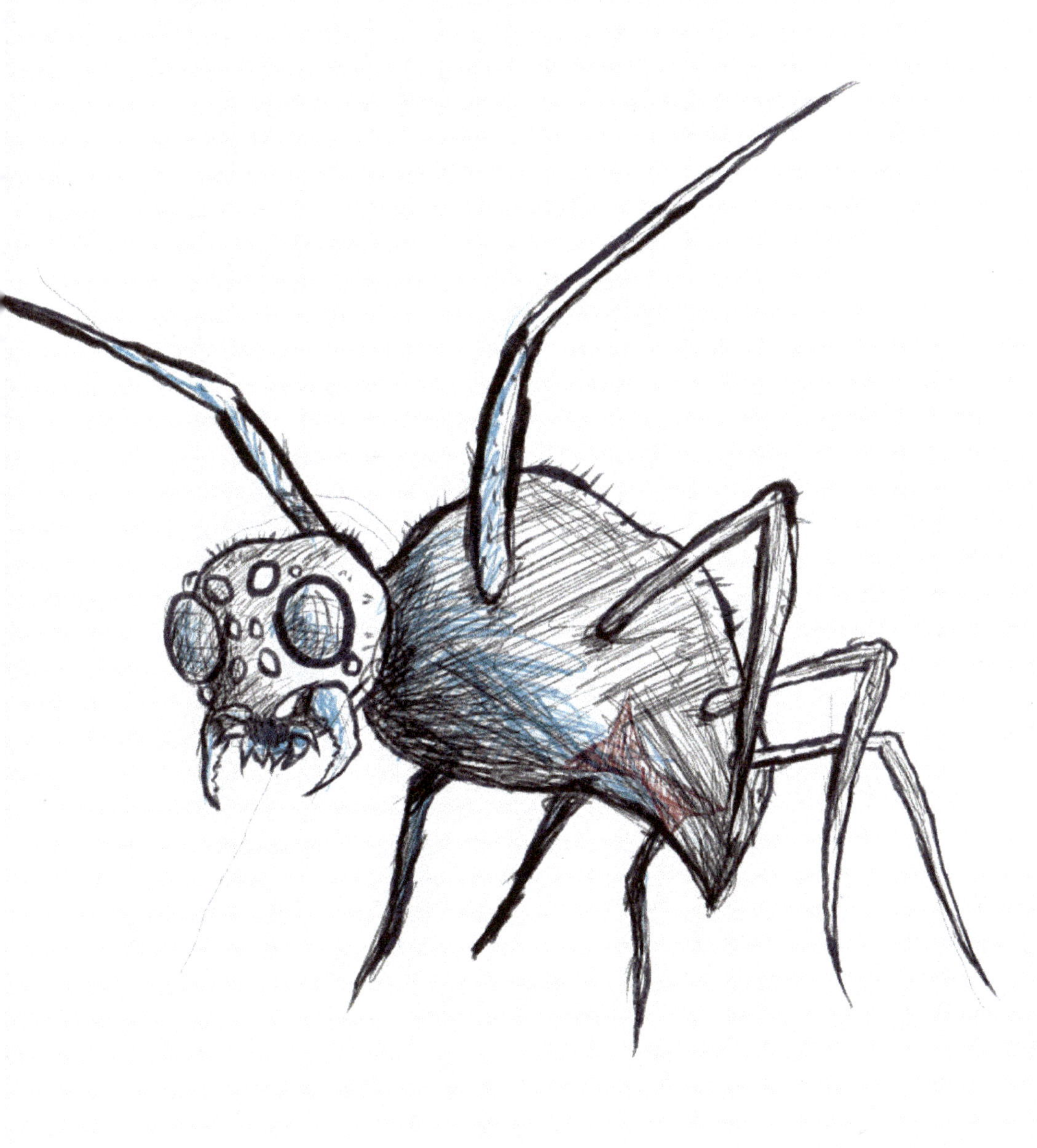

DAY III
PATH

On Day III, the theme "PATH" guided my pen as it traced the contours of a dirt path stretching into the horizon. With deliberate strokes, I sought to convey the quiet allure of a journey yet untaken. The barren trees, bereft of leaves, stood as silent witnesses to the passage of time, casting shadows along the path. As the ink flowed, the sketch unfolded like a visual metaphor, capturing the essence of choices made and the anticipation of what lies ahead. The simplicity of the scene echoed the profound nature of pathways, both literal and metaphorical, and served as a visual meditation on the inexorable march of time and the evolving landscapes of our own personal journeys. Day III, with its tranquil depiction, marked a contemplative pause in this creative sojourn.

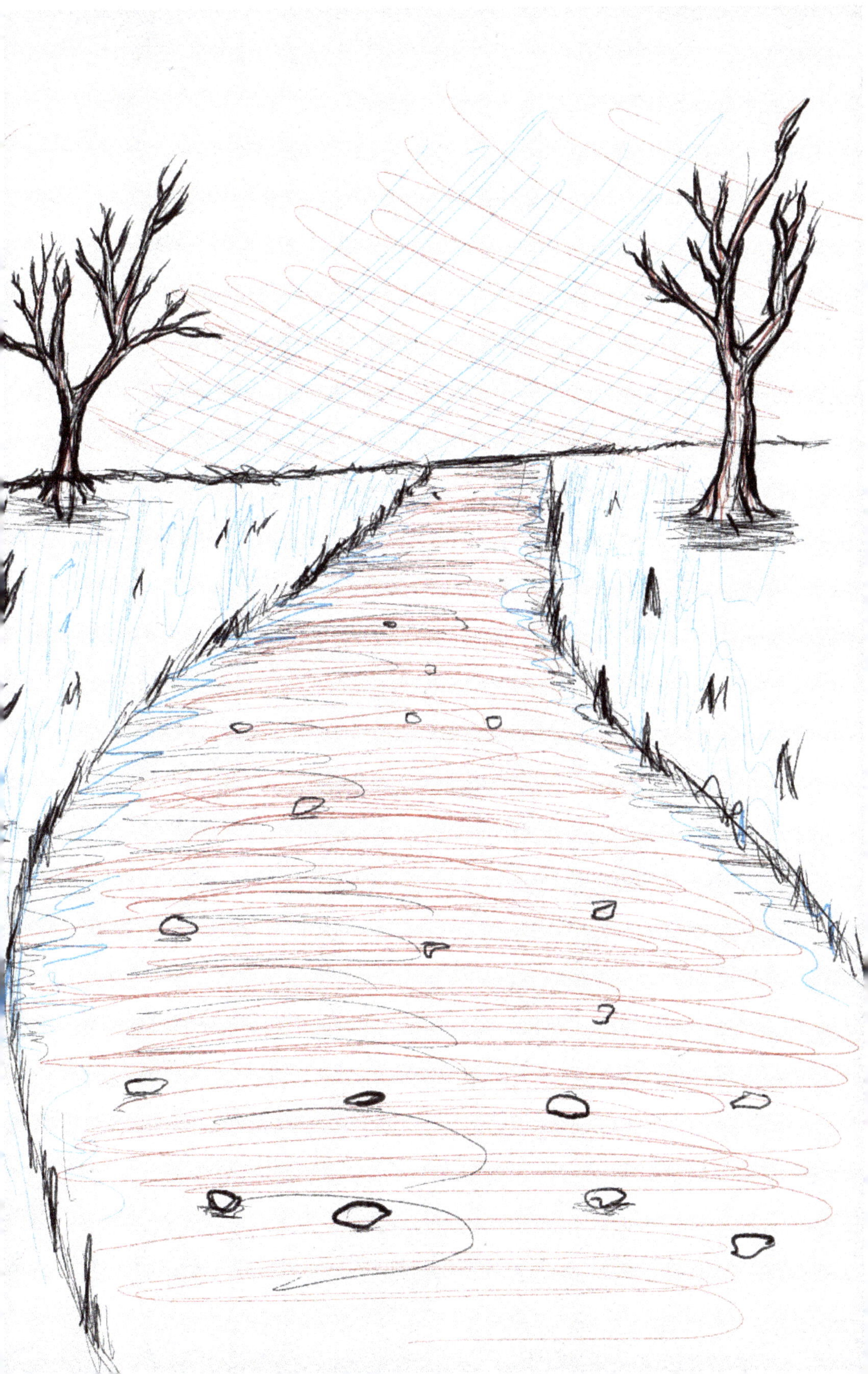

DAY IV
DODGE

On Day IV, the theme "DODGE" sparked a playful twist in my
artistic repertoire. In response, I sketched a dynamic scene
featuring a spirited man mid-dodge, evoking the lively chaos of
a dodgeball game. The animated lines captured the agility and
anticipation as the dodgeball whizzed through the air. This light-
hearted portrayal not only embraced the theme but also injected
a sense of energy and spontaneity into the creative narrative.
Day IV stands as a vibrant interlude, a departure from the serene
landscapes of previous days, reminding me of the delightful
versatility that artistic exploration can unveil within the
boundaries of a single word.

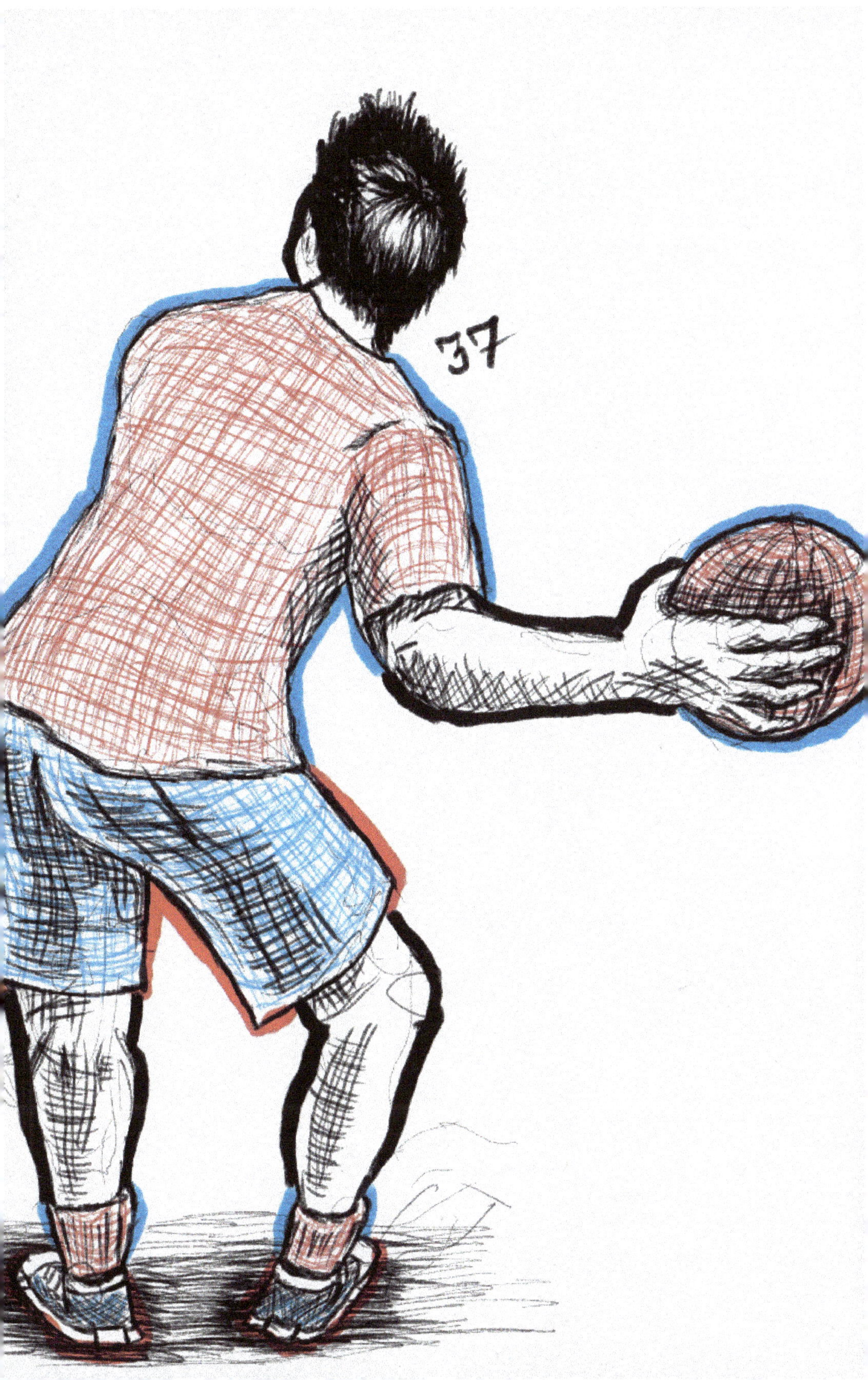
37

DAY V
MAP

For Day V, the evocative theme "MAP" led my pen to craft an intriguing island scene reminiscent of a pirate's treasure map. With a touch of whimsy, I outlined coastlines, added cryptic symbols, and adorned the imaginary land. The ink unfolded to weave a narrative of hidden treasures, uncharted waters, and the allure of adventure. The pirate map, with its enigmatic details, beckons the viewer to embark on a journey of exploration and discovery. Day V emerged as a delightful voyage into the realm of cartographic imagination, where every stroke carried the spirit of an untold story waiting to be unraveled.

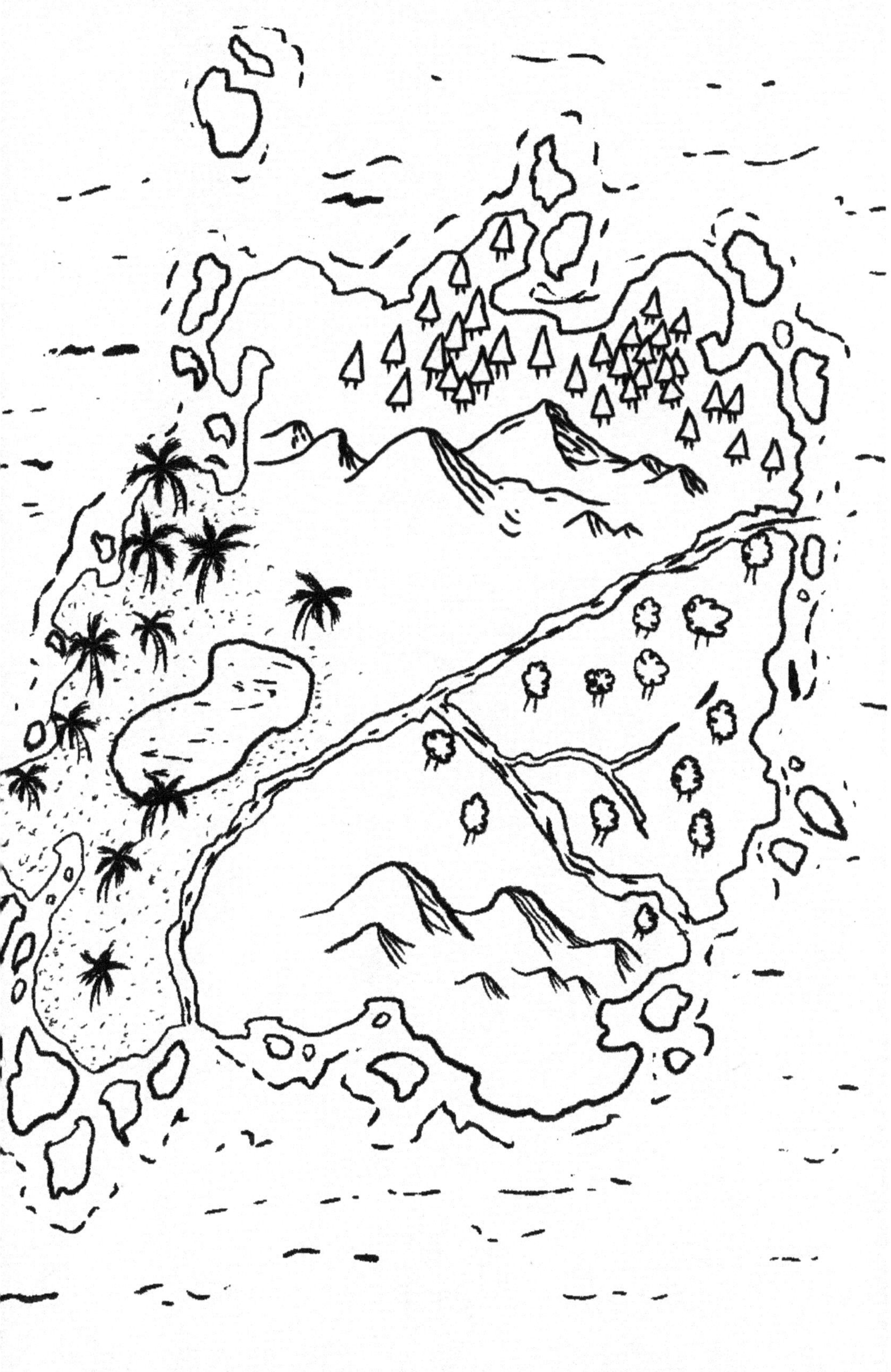

DAY VI
GOLDEN

On Day VI, the theme "GOLDEN" became the guiding light for my artistic endeavor, inspiring the creation of a lively sketch featuring a golden retriever. With careful strokes, I sought to capture the radiant warmth of this beloved canine companion, its fur illuminated by a golden glow. The playful spirit of the golden retriever leapt from the paper, inviting viewers to share in the joy and exuberance of a faithful friend. Day VI unfolded as a celebration of the precious moments found in the company of our four-legged companions, embodying the essence of "golden" in the form of unconditional love and boundless happiness.

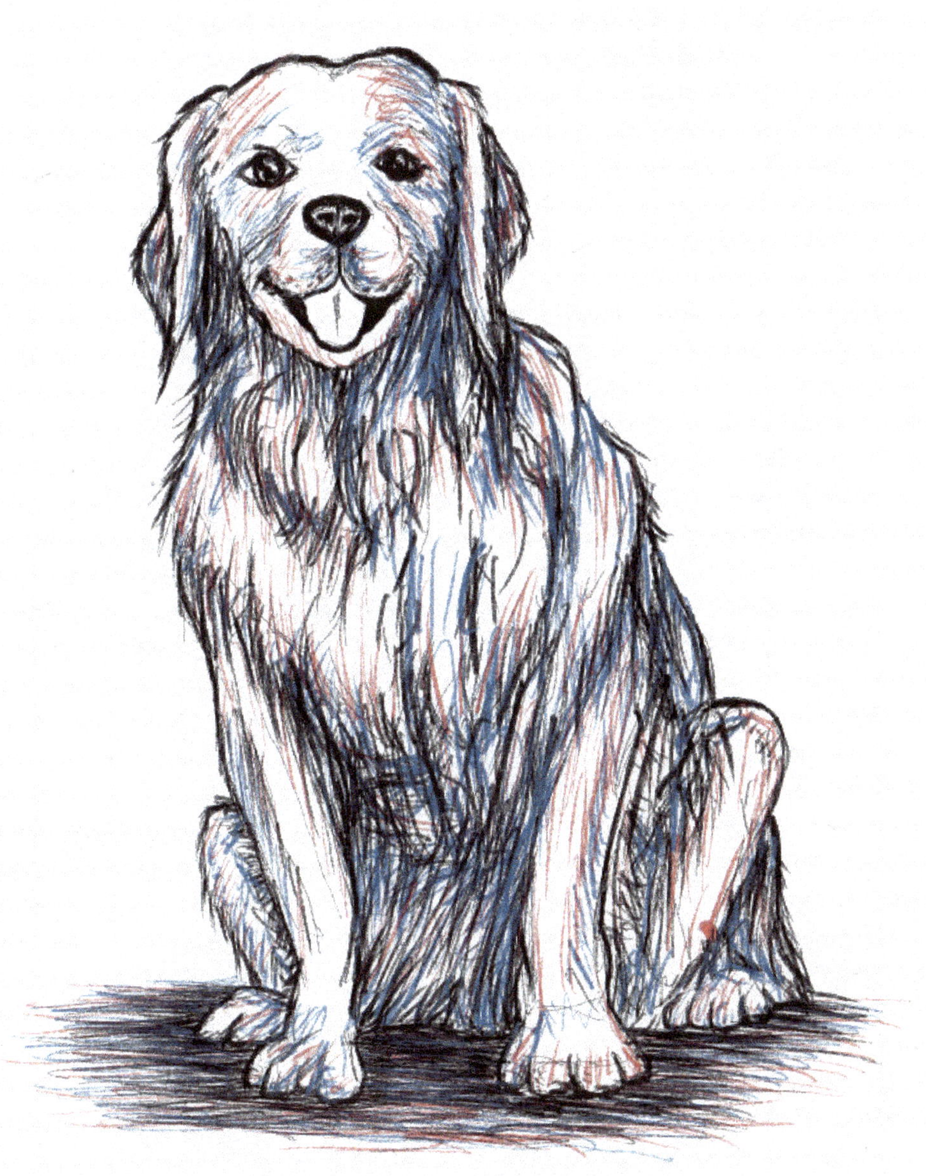

DAY VII
DRIP

On Day VII, the theme "DRIP" led my pen to cascade across the canvas, forming a visually striking representation of the word itself. The letters, captured mid-drip, conveyed a sense of fluidity and motion. The inked typography echoed the dynamic nature of the theme, creating an illusion of letters melting and reforming. Day VII's exploration of the "DRIP" theme became an artistic experiment in capturing movement and transformation within the confines of a single word, allowing the ink to take on a life of its own and imbue the artwork with a sense of energetic spontaneity.

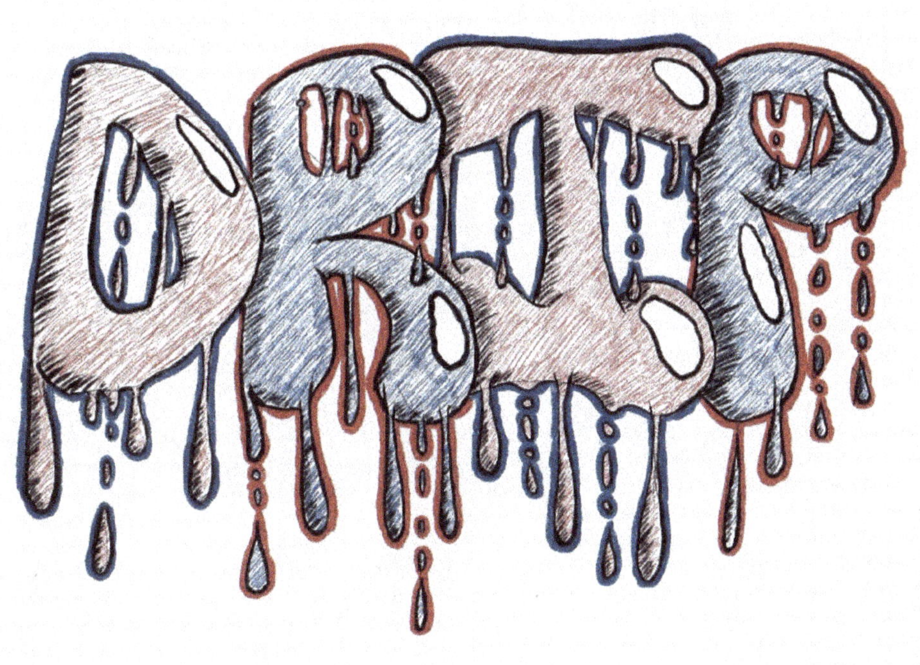

DAY VIII
TOAD

For Day VIII, the theme "TOAD" guided my artistic expression as I brought to life the charming presence of a toad or frog on paper. With a careful interplay of lines and shading, the amphibian emerged, its webbed feet perched on an imagined lily pad. The inked rendition sought to capture the intricate textures of its skin and the whimsical nature of these fascinating creatures. Day VIII unfolded as a homage to the quiet beauty found in the natural world, celebrating the unassuming yet captivating charm of toads that often dwell in the overlooked corners of our surroundings.

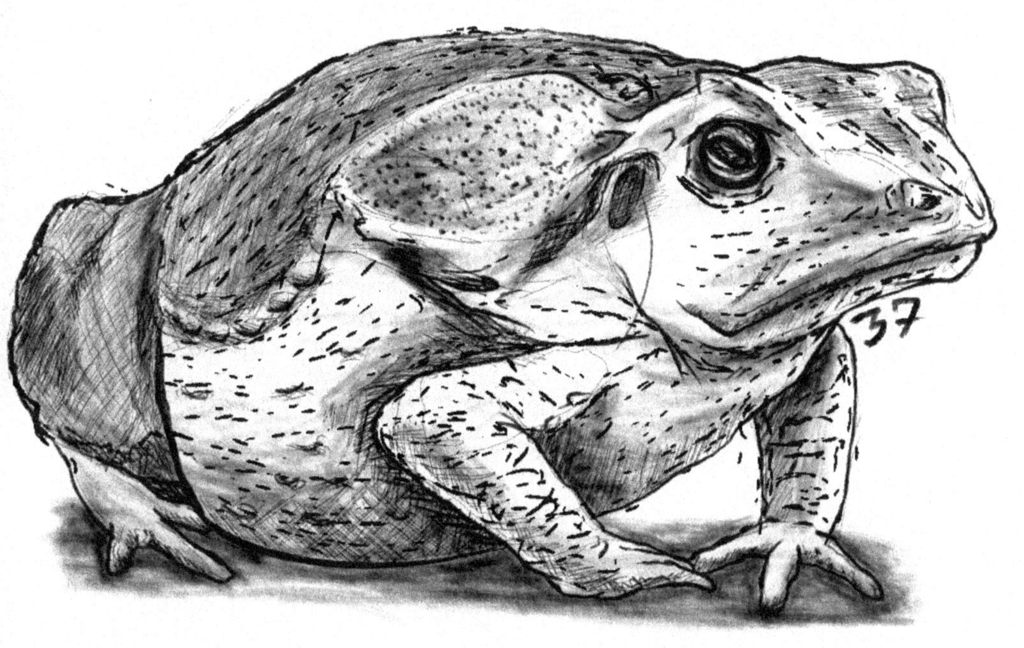

DAY IX
BOUNCE

On Day IX, the theme "BOUNCE" inspired a lively and dynamic creation as I sketched bouncing text, injecting a sense of movement into the very essence of the word. Each letter appeared to leap and rebound, capturing the spirited energy associated with the theme. The inked typography echoed the playful nature of bouncing, adding a visual bounce to the letters themselves. Day IX unfolded as a visual celebration of the theme, transforming a static word into a vibrant, animated representation that echoed the joyful cadence of boundless enthusiasm.

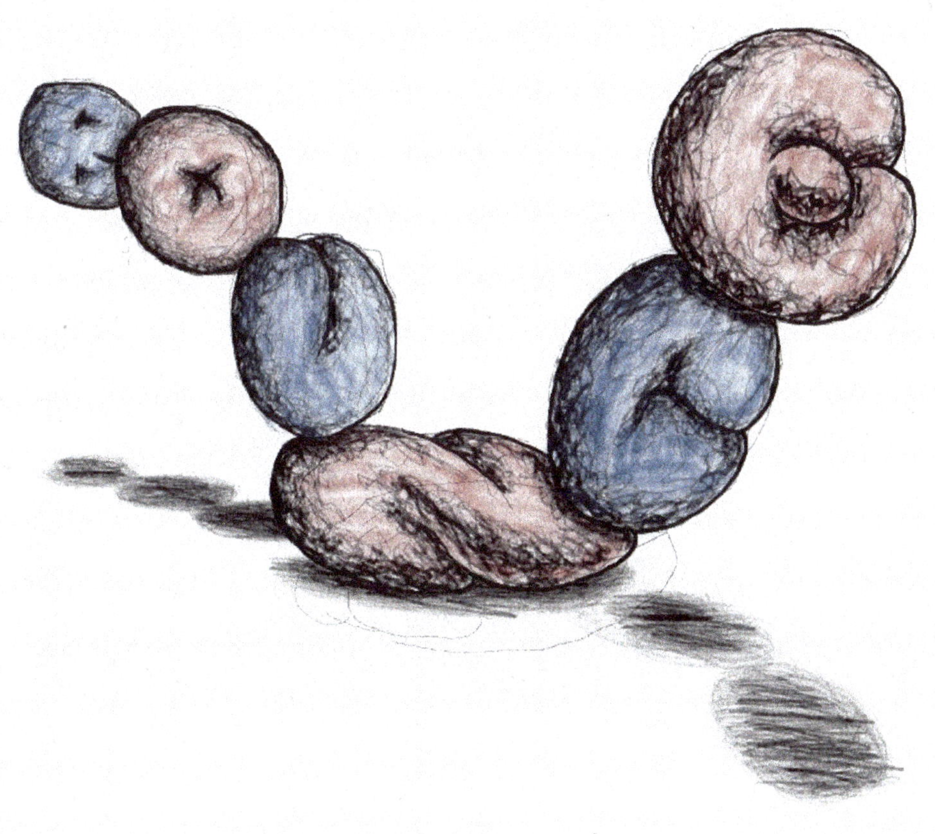

DAY X
FORTUNE

On Day X, the theme "FORTUNE" prompted the creation of a captivating scene as I sketched a slot machine. Each reel was adorned with symbols of luck, promising the anticipation and thrill of fortune with every spin. The inked depiction aimed to capture the glimmering lights and the excitement of a moment that holds the promise of unexpected wealth. Day X unfolded as a visual exploration of the whims of chance and the allure of fortune, encapsulating the essence of luck and risk in the symbolic dance of the slot machine's reels.

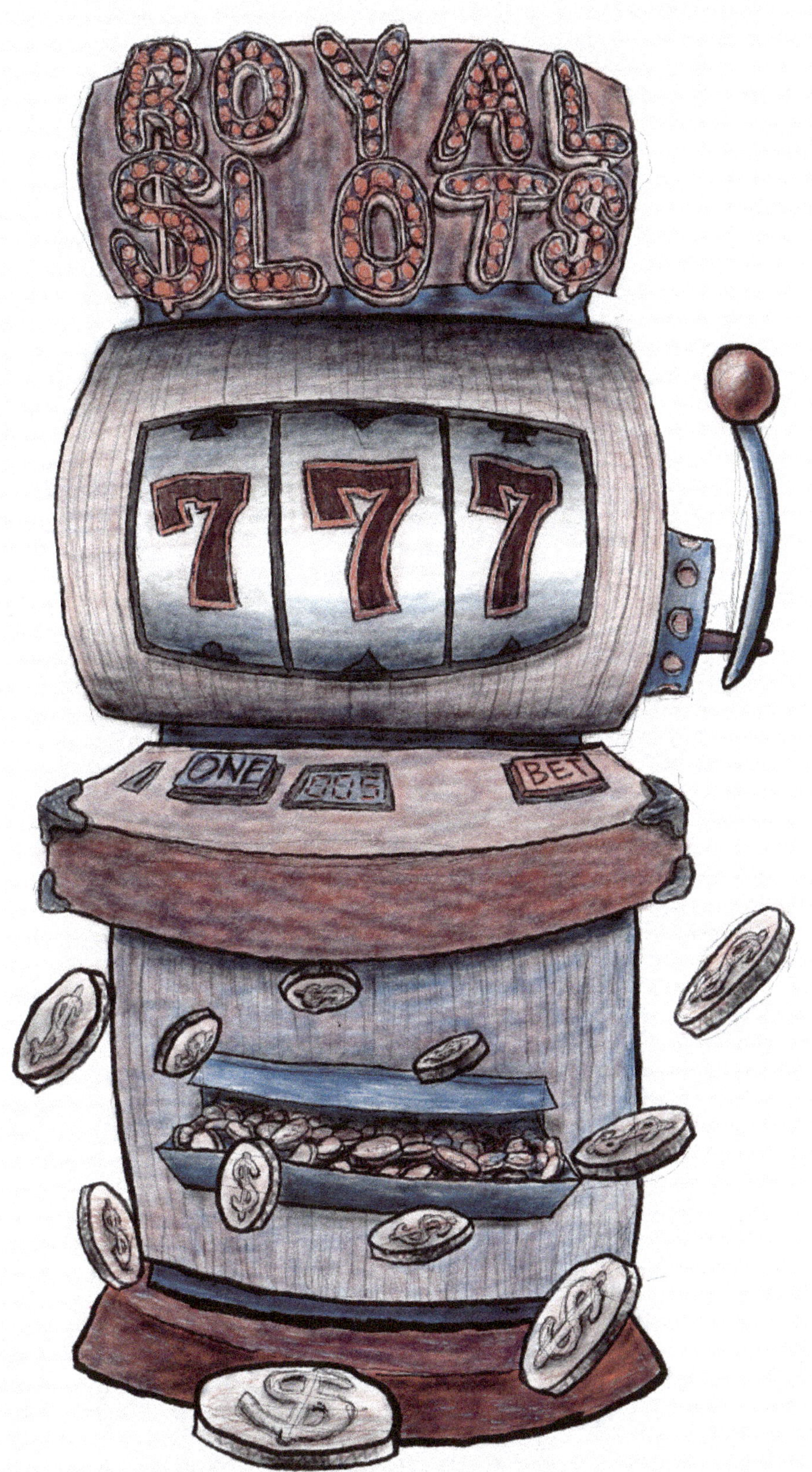

ROYAL LOT
7 7 7
ONE
BET

DAY XI
WANDER

On Day XI, the theme "WANDER" guided my pen to depict a contemplative scene of a lone figure lost in thought as he traverses an undefined path. The sketch captured the essence of wandering—a journey without a predetermined destination, driven by curiosity and a sense of exploration. The intricacies of the wandering man's posture and the undetermined landscape around him told a visual story of introspection and the beauty found in the meandering journey itself. Day XI unfolded as a poignant exploration of the wanderer's spirit, inviting viewers to join in the quiet contemplation of the boundless possibilities that unfold with each step into the unknown.

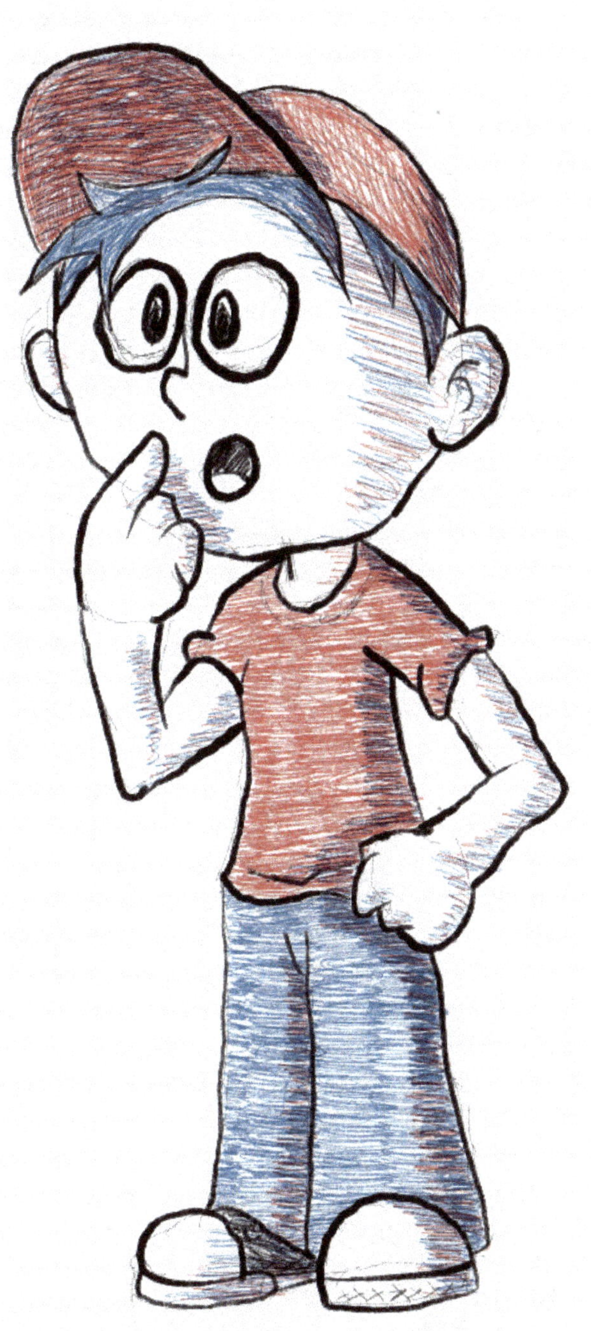

DAY XII
SPICEY

On Day XII, the theme "SPICY" ignited my creative vision, leading me to sketch a vibrant and fiery representation of a red pepper. The inked illustration captured the essence of heat and intensity, as flames danced around the pepper, symbolizing the fiery nature of spiciness. The vivid portrayal aimed to evoke not only the visual appeal of the red pepper but also the sensory experience of its spicy flavor. Day XII unfolded as a visual feast, celebrating the bold and intense character of spice, encapsulated in the dynamic image of a red pepper ablaze with flavorful intensity.

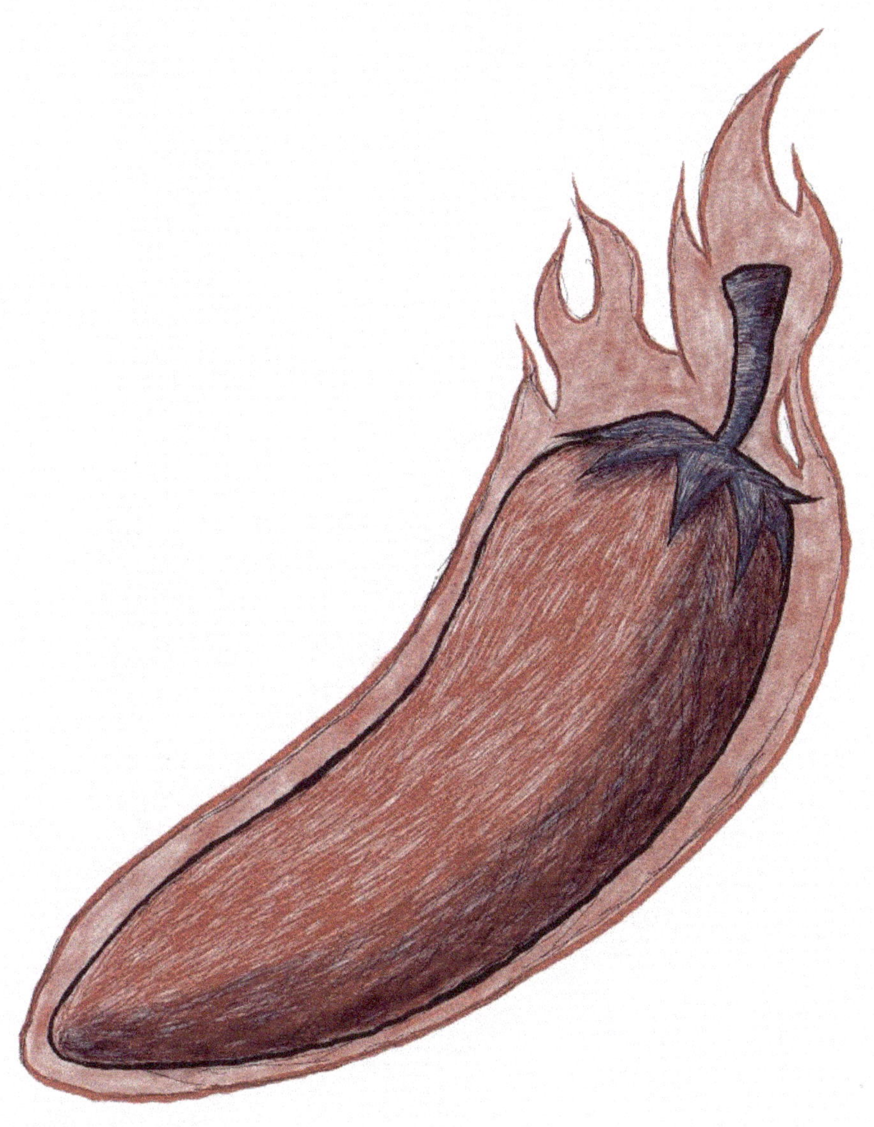

DAY XIII
RISE

On Day XIII, the theme "RISE" propelled my artistic expression to new heights as I sketched a captivating scene of a rocketship ascending beyond the bounds of Earth. The inked illustration captured the spirit of ascent, portraying the powerful thrust of engines and the dynamic journey of leaving our home planet. The soaring rocket symbolized not only physical elevation but also the ambitious pursuit of dreams and exploration. Day XIII unfolded as a visual ode to the unyielding human spirit, reaching for the stars and rising above earthly confines in an awe-inspiring quest for the unknown.

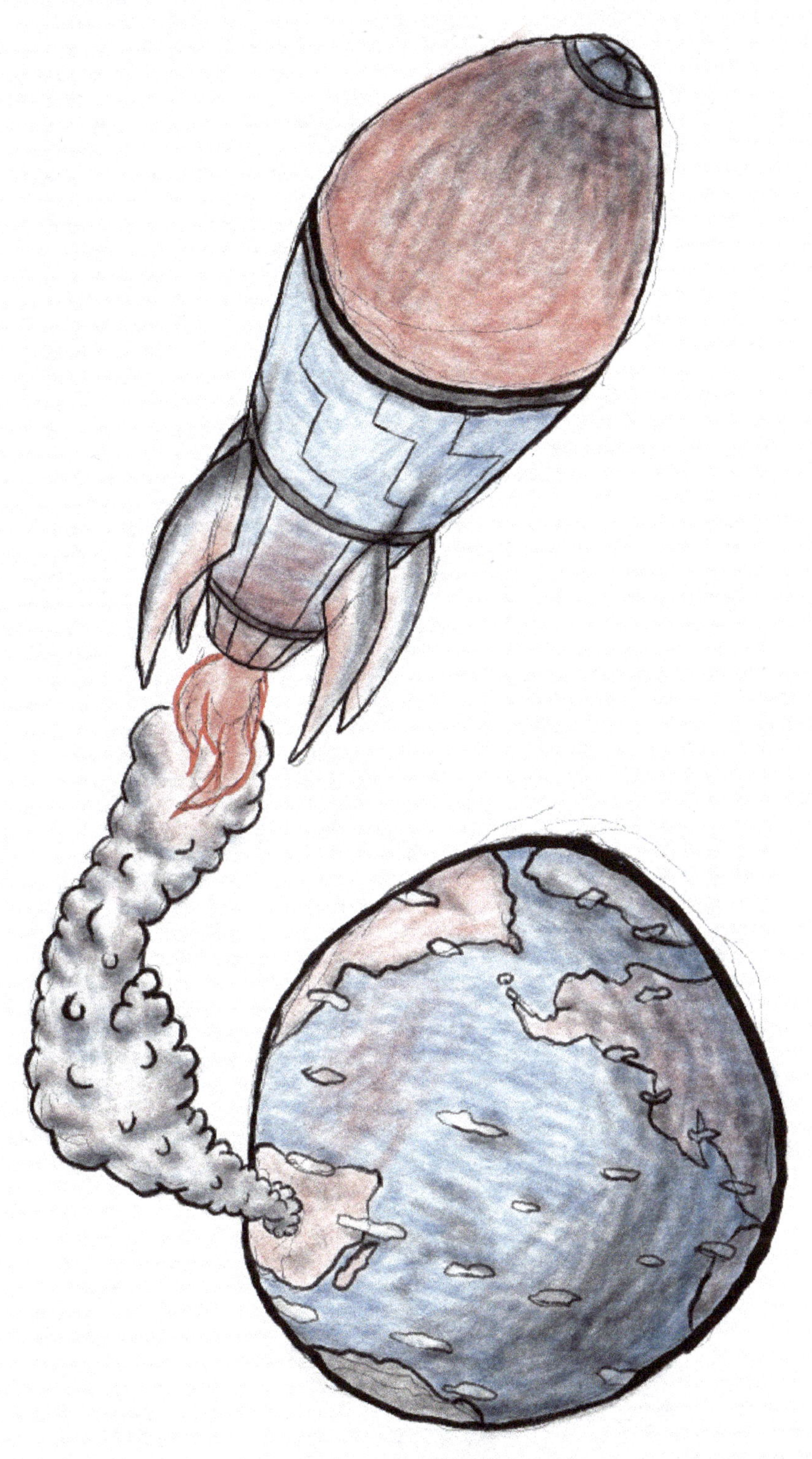

DAY XIV
CASTLE

On Day XIV, the theme "CASTLE" invited me to immerse my pen in the rich history of medieval architecture, resulting in the creation of a detailed sketch featuring a towering castle reminiscent of a bygone era. The inked illustration captured the grandeur of stone walls, turrets, and battlements, evoking the timeless allure of medieval fortresses. The meticulous lines aimed to transport viewers to a realm of knights, royalty, and enchantment. Day XIV unfolded as a visual journey through the pages of history, celebrating the enduring charm and majesty of the medieval castle, a symbol of strength and romance that stands defiant against the passage of time.

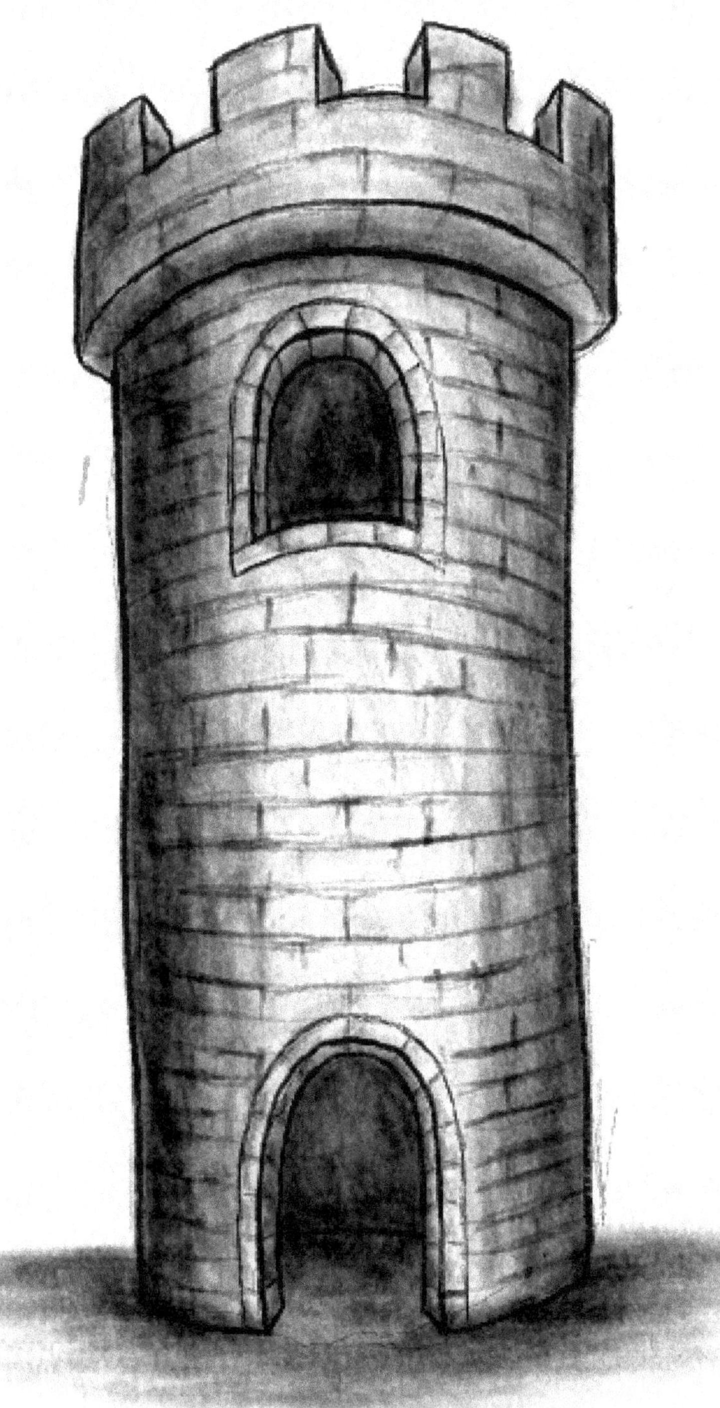

DAY XV
DAGGER

On Day XV, the theme "DAGGER" prompted the emergence of a powerful and intricately detailed sketch, featuring a sharp and formidable dagger. The inked illustration sought to capture the sleek and lethal nature of this weapon, with meticulous attention to its hilt, blade, and overall design. The lines conveyed a sense of precision and danger, encapsulating the essence of the theme. Day XV unfolded as a visual exploration of the symbolic and historical significance of the dagger, a potent representation of both elegance and peril, evoking the dual nature that lies within such a weapon.

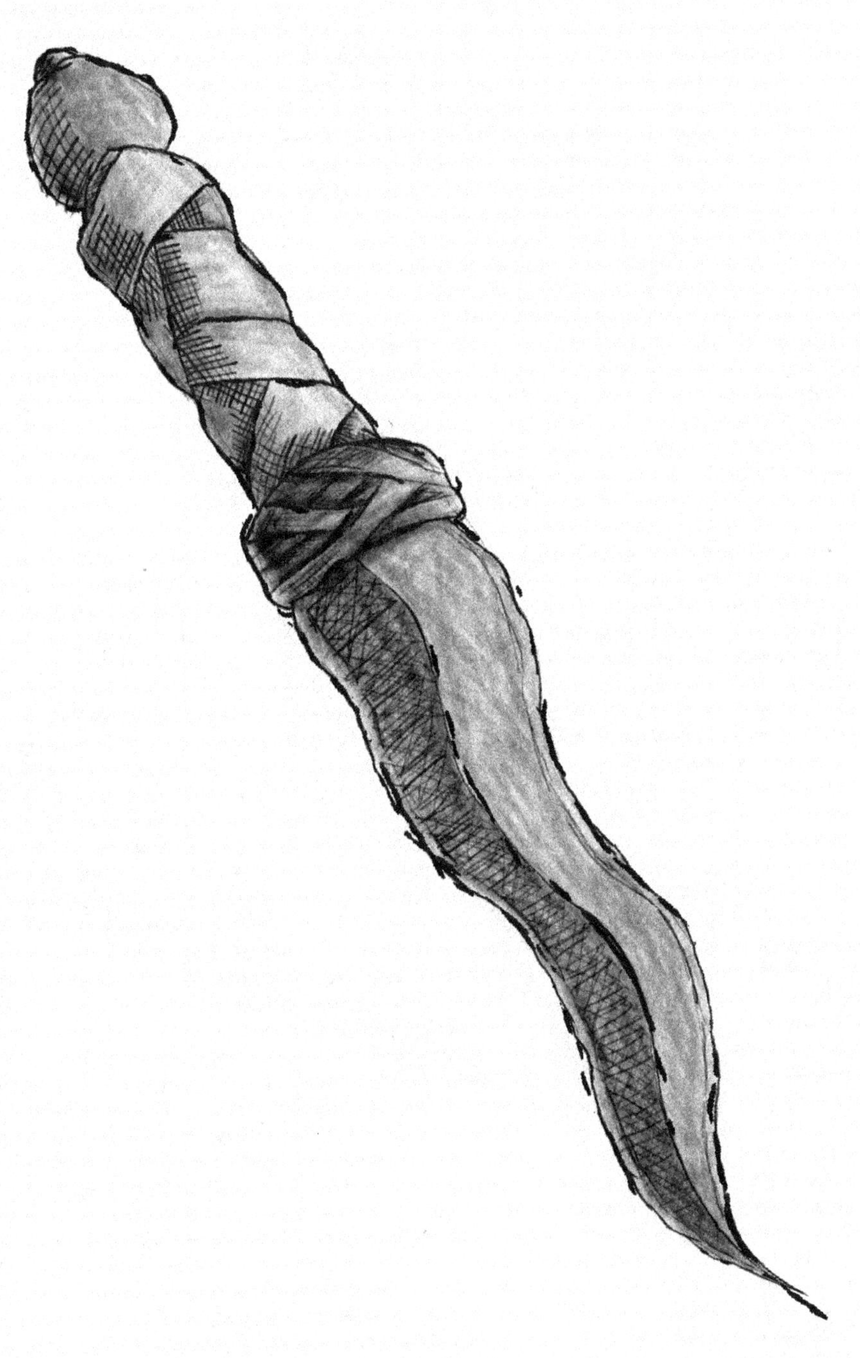

DAY XVI
ANGEL

On Day XVI, the theme "ANGEL" inspired a whimsical and heartwarming creation as my pen brought forth the image of a joyous ghost spirit with the essence of an angel. The inked illustration portrayed the ethereal being with a light-hearted and celestial demeanor, capturing the spirit's contentment and grace. The fusion of angelic qualities with the playful nature of a ghost resulted in a unique character, radiating a sense of warmth and positivity. Day XVI unfolded as a visual celebration of the supernatural, blending the ethereal and the cheerful into a harmonious representation of an angelic presence with a delightful twist.

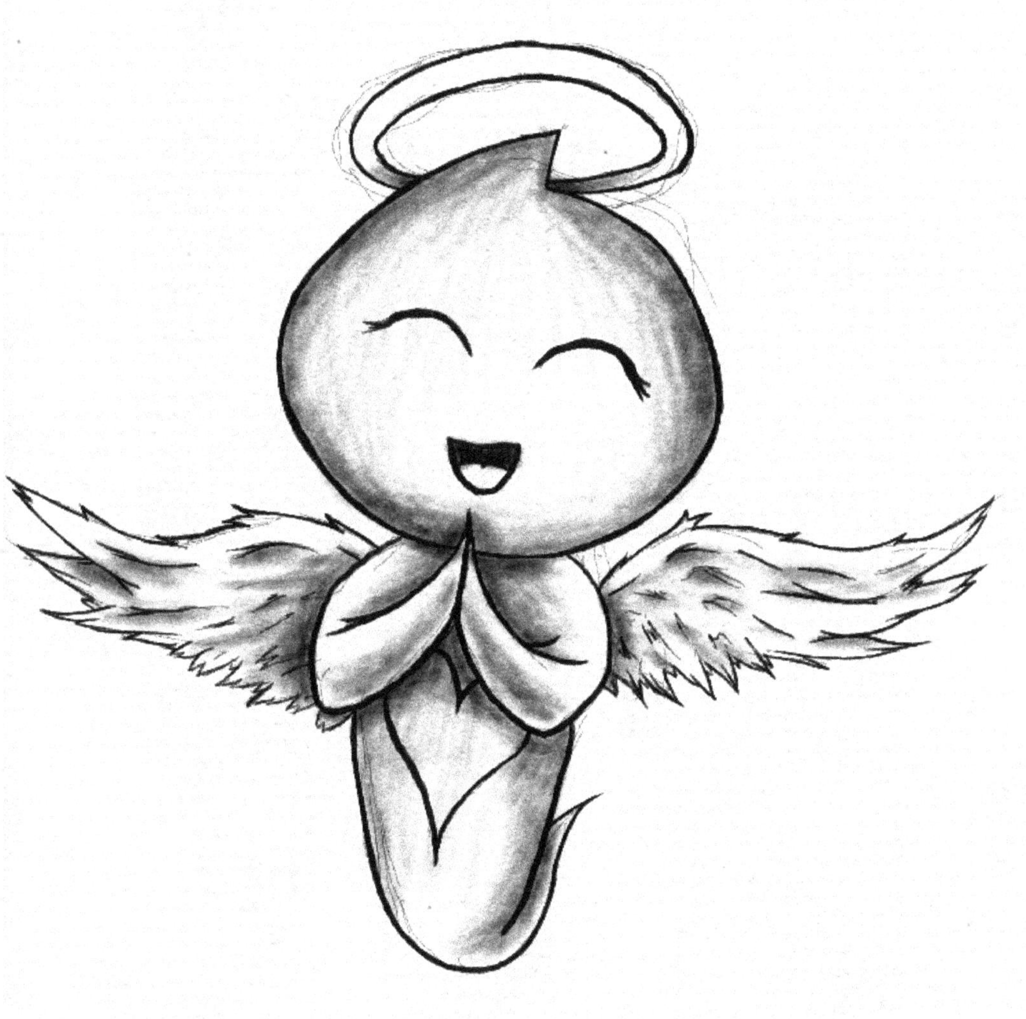

DAY XVII
DEMON

On Day XVII, the theme "DEMON" led my pen to conjure a dark and formidable spirit with an aura of malevolence. The inked illustration depicted the demon with sharp features, ominous shadows, and an overall presence that conveyed a sense of foreboding. This visual exploration delved into the darker realms of the supernatural, contrasting the ethereal joy of the previous day's angelic spirit. Day XVII unfolded as a captivating study of duality, showcasing the coexistence of light and shadow within the realm of spirits and transcendent beings. The demon, with its fierce countenance, added a touch of mystery and intrigue to this ongoing visual narrative.

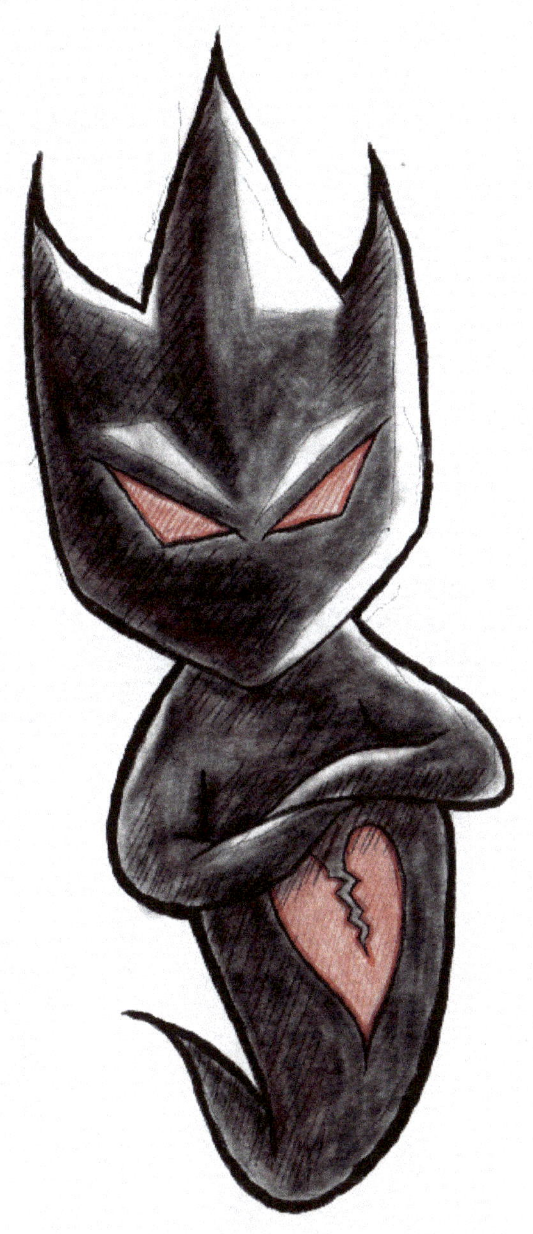

XVIII
SADDLE

On Day XVIII, the theme "SADDLE" spurred my artistic imagination, leading to the creation of a sketch featuring a majestic horse. The inked illustration captured the graceful form of the equine companion, adorned with a saddle, ready for adventure. The carefully rendered details of the horse and saddle conveyed a sense of strength, elegance, and the spirit of exploration. Day XVIII unfolded as a visual ode to the bond between rider and steed, encapsulating the timeless connection forged through the art of riding and the symbiotic relationship between human and horse.

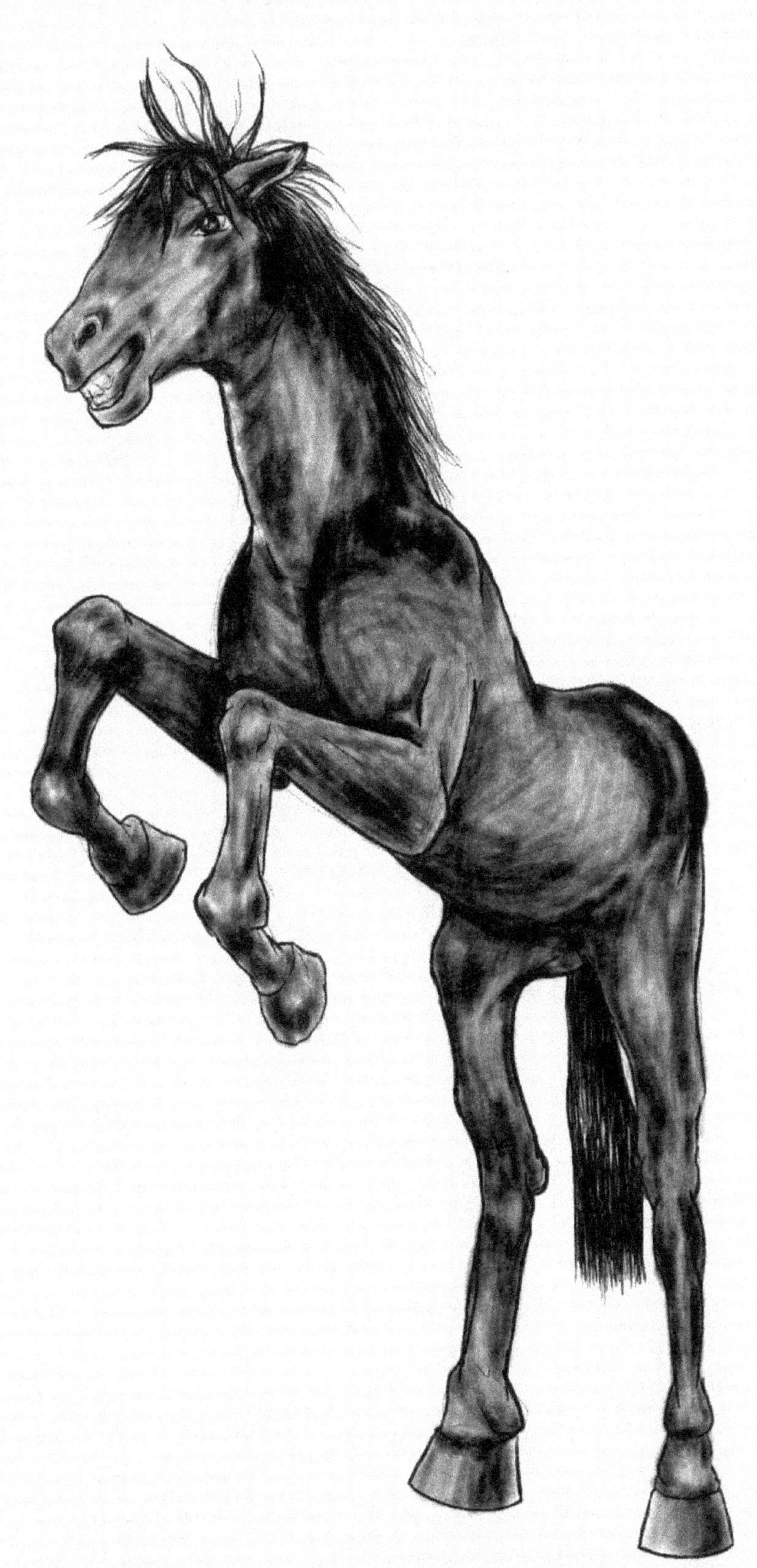

DAY XIX
PLUMP

On Day XIX, the theme "PLUMP" inspired a delightful and endearing sketch featuring a charming pig. The inked illustration highlighted the rotund and plump nature of the pig, capturing its adorable essence. With careful strokes, the portrayal conveyed not only the physical attributes of plumpness but also the inherent charm and personality of the porcine subject. Day XIX unfolded as a visual celebration of the whimsical and cuddly side of the animal kingdom, inviting viewers to appreciate the simple joy found in the plump and lovable presence of a contented pig.

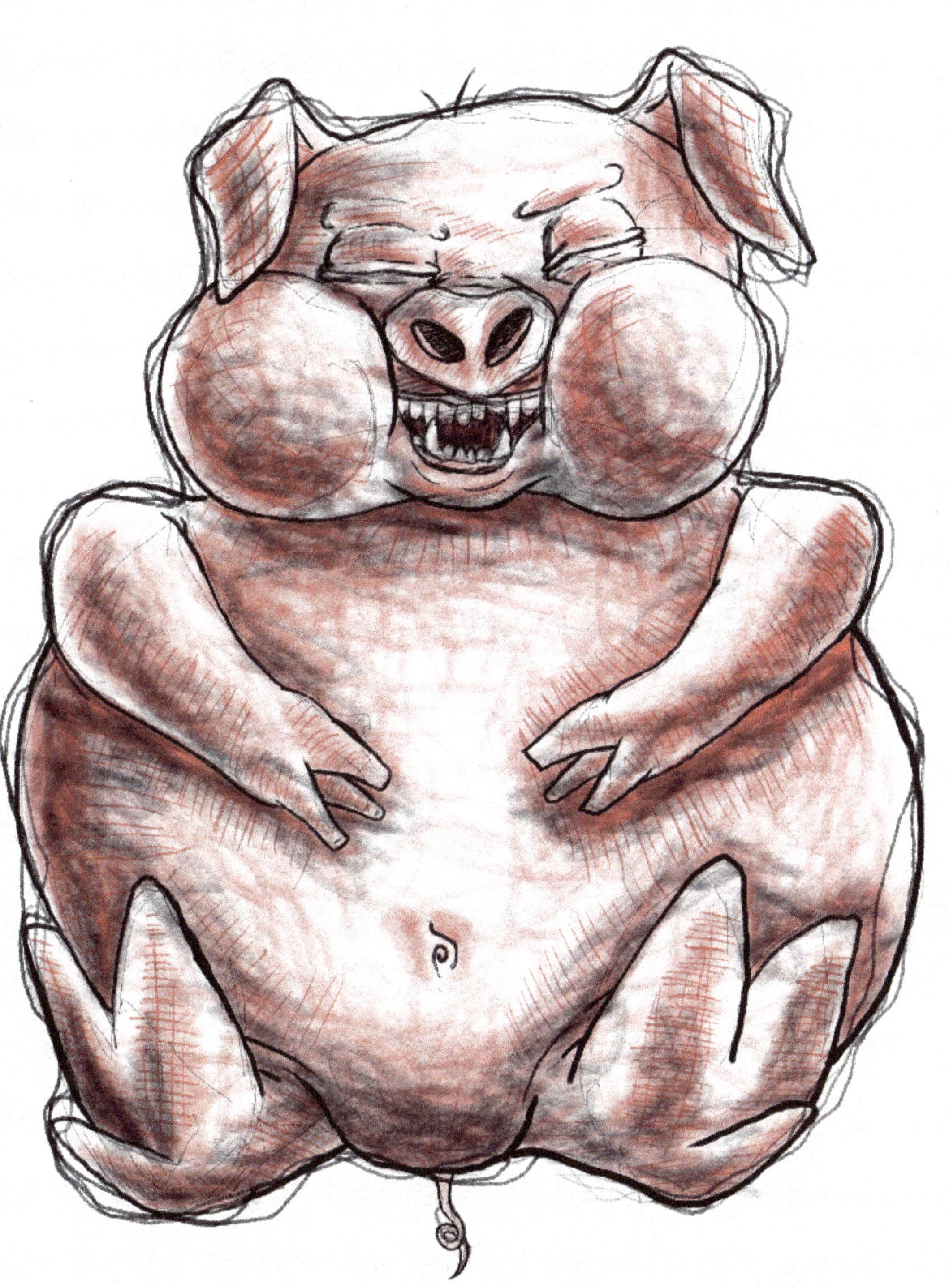

DAY XX
FROST

On Day XX, the theme "FROST" led my pen to create a wintry scene as I sketched a cheerful snowman. The inked illustration captured the essence of frosty delight, depicting the snowman adorned with a carrot nose, coal eyes, and a welcoming grin. The details of the scene conveyed the playful and magical atmosphere of a winter's day. Day XX unfolded as a visual ode to the enchantment of frosty landscapes, evoking the timeless joy associated with building snowmen and reveling in the whimsical beauty of a winter wonderland.

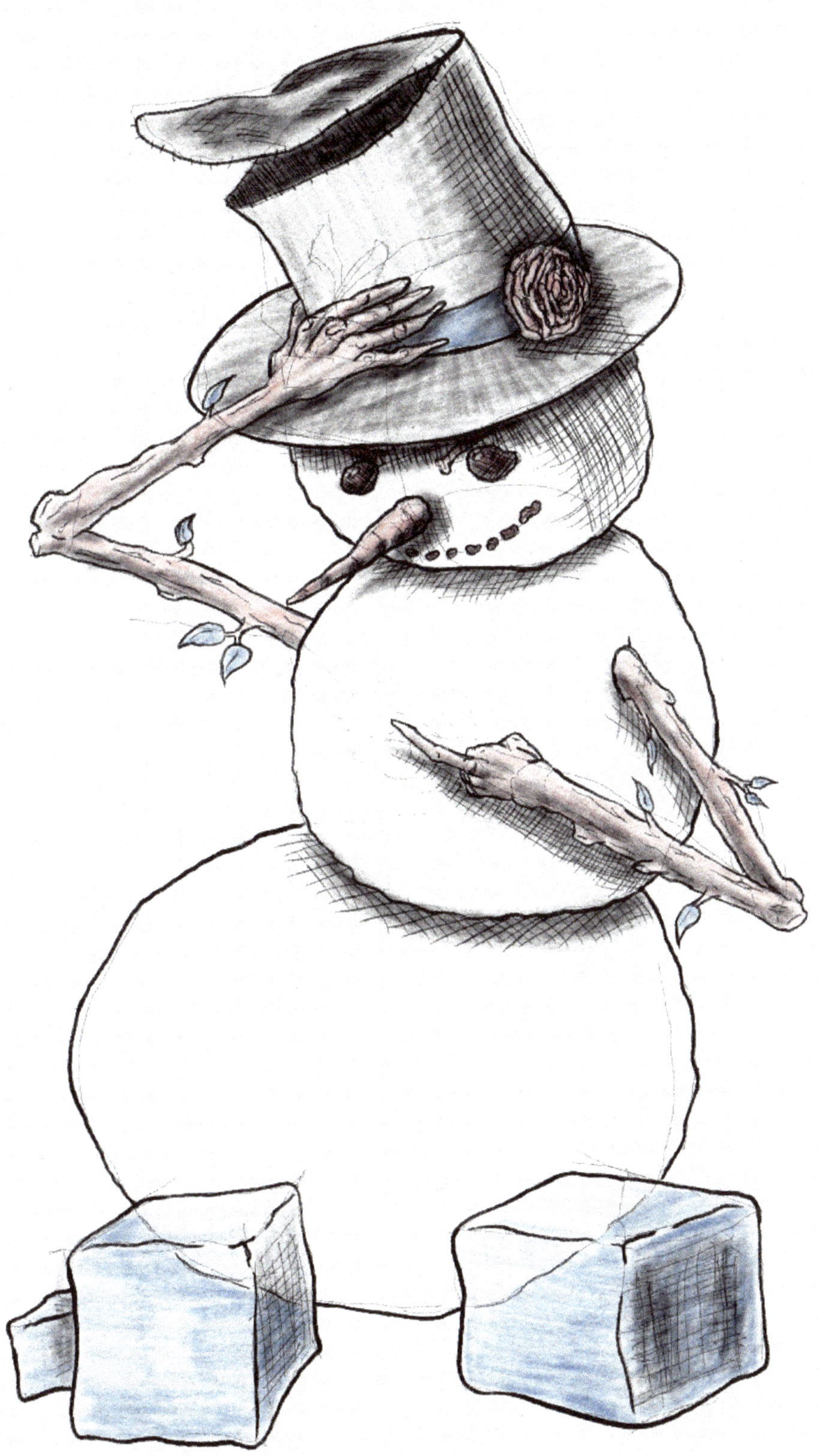

DAY XXI
CHAINS

On Day XXI, the theme "CHAINS" inspired a powerful and symbolic sketch featuring a circle of interlinked chains. The inked illustration conveyed a sense of strength, unity, and interconnectedness, as the chains formed a protective and unbroken ring. The details of each link told a story of resilience and collaboration, suggesting a collective strength that transcends individual components. Day XXI unfolded as a visual exploration of the profound symbolism of chains, highlighting the potential for unity, solidarity, and the strength that arises when individuals come together to form an unyielding circle of support.

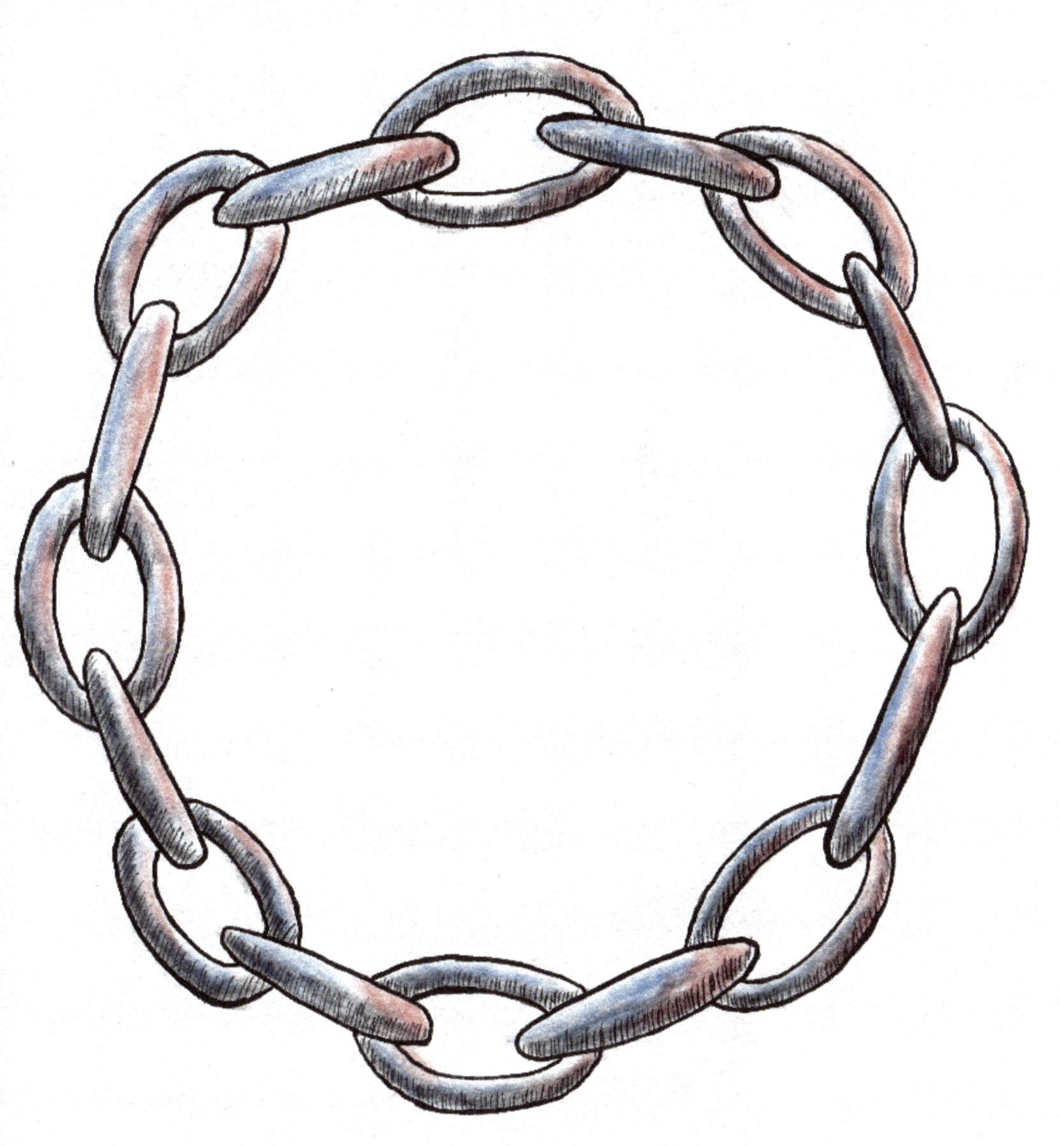

DAY XXII
SCRATCHY

On Day XXII, the theme "SCRATCHY" guided my pen to create a whimsical and charming sketch featuring a chicken. Embracing the playful notion of "chicken scratch," the inked illustration depicted the feathery friend with a delightful, scratchy quality to its lines. The character of the chicken came to life with a lighthearted and endearing touch, capturing the essence of spontaneity and charm. Day XXII unfolded as a visual celebration of the creative spirit, infusing the concept of "scratchiness" with a feathered friend's cheerful presence, adding a delightful twist to the ongoing artistic journey.

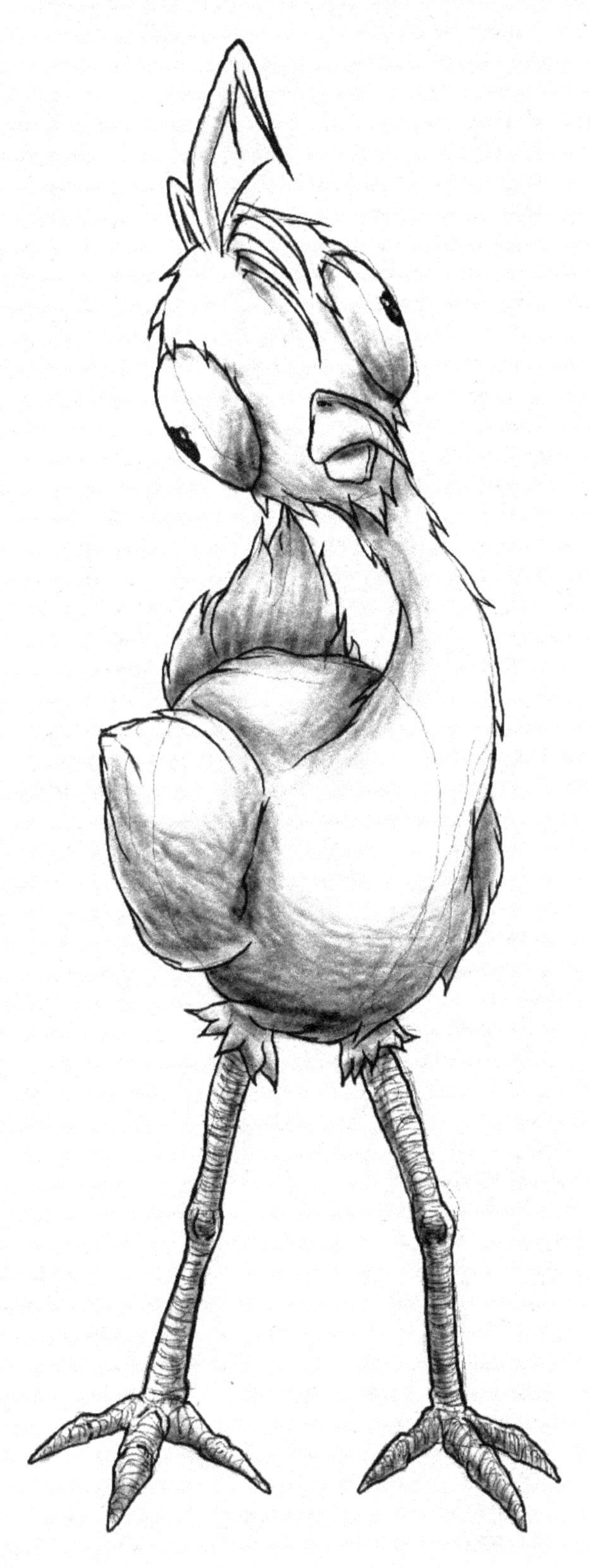

DAY XXIII
CELESTIAL

On Day XXIII, the theme "CELESTIAL" sparked an extraterrestrial exploration as my pen sketched a UFO beaming up an alien. The inked illustration captured the otherworldly essence of the celestial scene, depicting the UFO with mysterious lights and the alien lifted in a beam of light. The details conveyed a sense of wonder and the unknown, inviting viewers to contemplate the mysteries of the cosmos. Day XXIII unfolded as a visual voyage into the celestial realms, blending science fiction with the enchantment of the stars, and offering a glimpse into the captivating and mysterious possibilities that lie beyond our earthly confines.

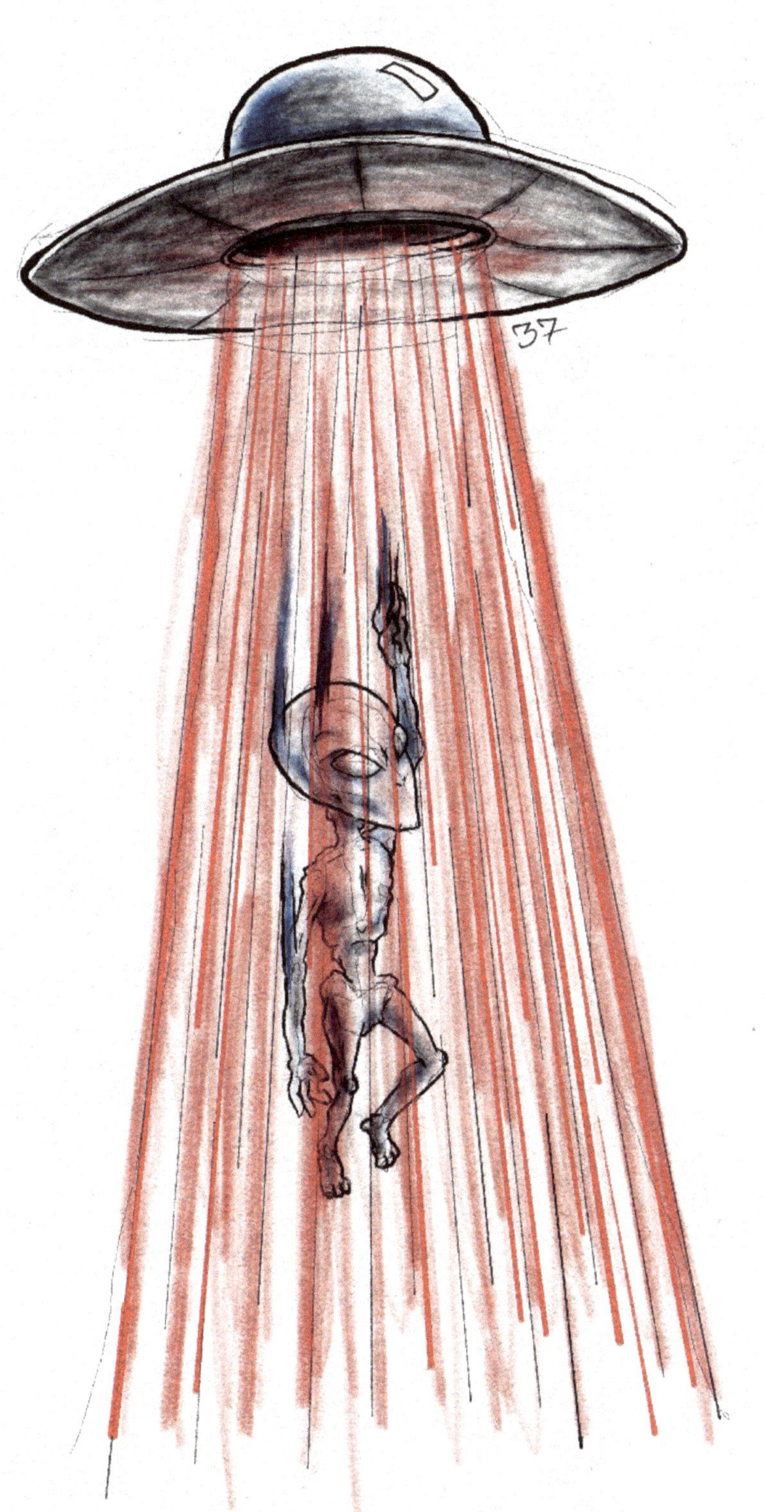

37

DAY XXIV
SHALLOW

On Day XXIV, the theme "SHALLOW" inspired a poignant and thought-provoking sketch featuring a goldfish in a fishbowl with low water. The inked illustration captured the vulnerability of the aquatic inhabitant, emphasizing the limited space within the bowl. The portrayal served as a visual metaphor, exploring the concept of shallowness in terms of confinement and restricted perspectives. Day XXIV unfolded as a reflection on the delicate balance between life and the confines of one's environment, inviting viewers to ponder the implications of living in shallow waters and the potential for growth beyond the limitations of a confined space.

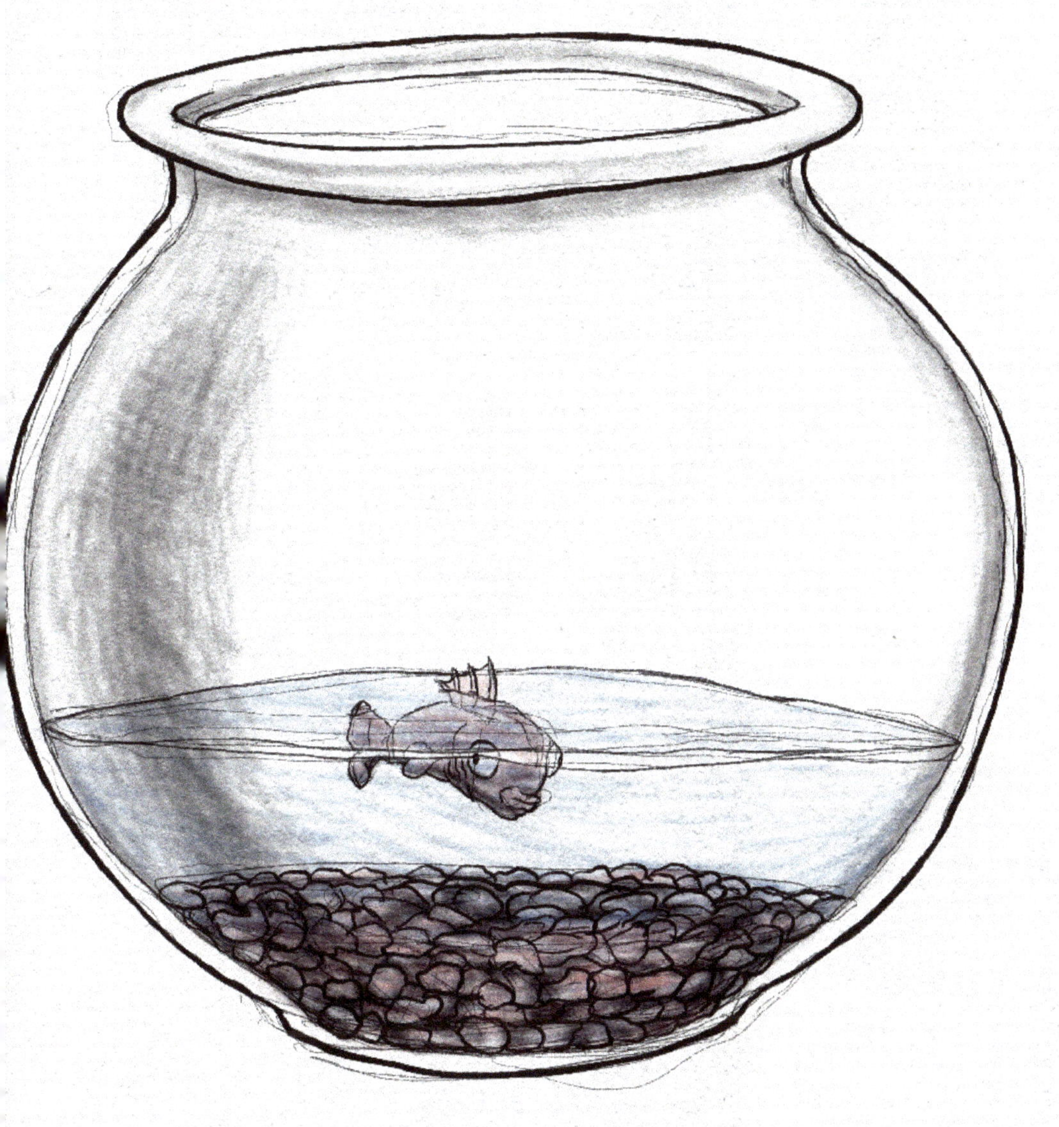

DAY XXV
DANGEROUS

On Day XXV, the theme "DANGEROUS" prompted a stark and impactful sketch featuring a syringe filled with drugs or pills. The inked illustration sought to convey the inherent risks and potential harm associated with substances that can be perilous to one's well-being. The stark imagery serves as a visual cautionary tale, inviting viewers to contemplate the dangers that may lurk within seemingly innocuous objects. Day XXV unfolded as a solemn exploration of the perilous nature of certain substances, highlighting the need for awareness and caution in the face of potentially harmful choices.

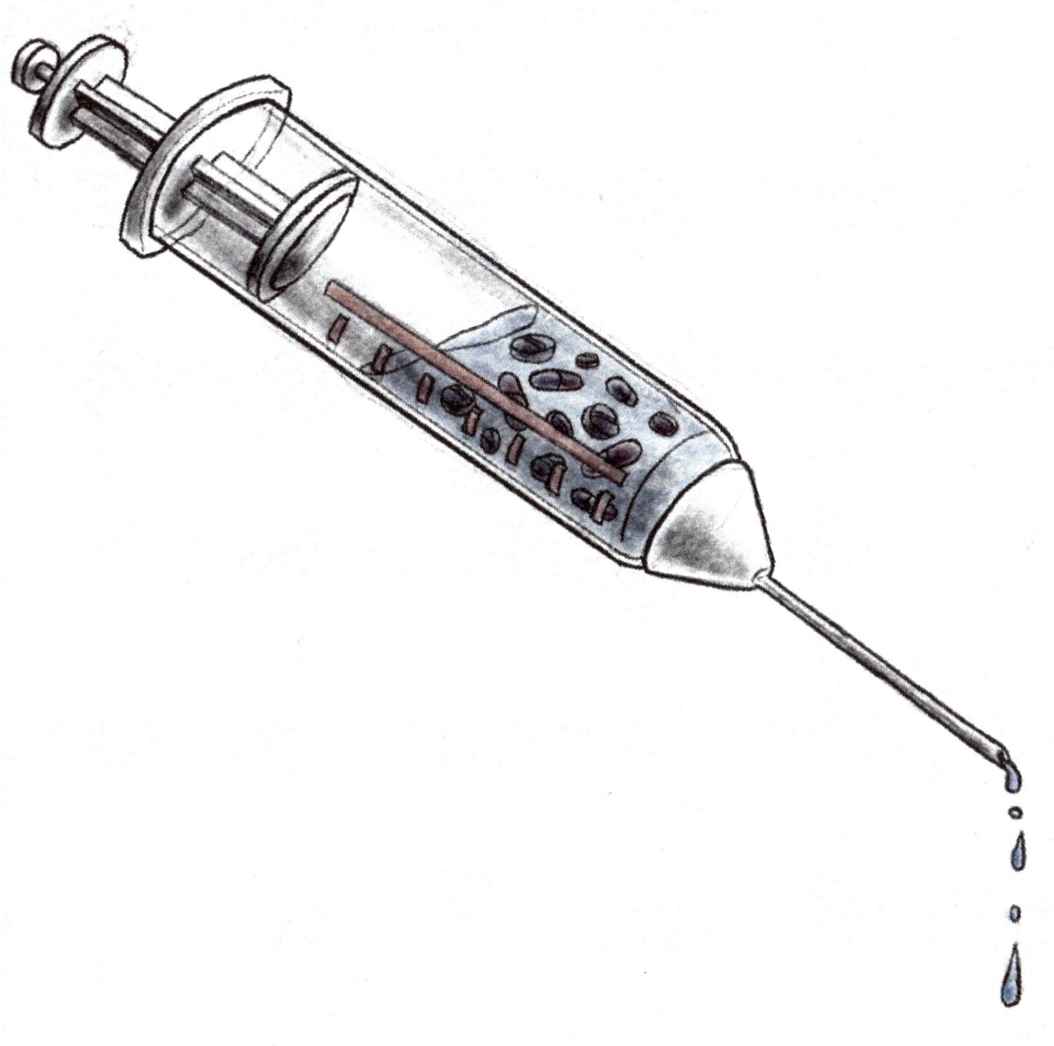

DAY XXVI
REMOVE

On Day XXVI, the theme "REMOVE" guided my pen to create a simple yet evocative sketch featuring an eraser. The inked illustration depicted the tool poised to remove pencil marks, capturing the essence of correction and elimination. The eraser, with its clean lines and purposeful placement, became a symbolic representation of the power to undo, rectify, and start anew. Day XXVI unfolded as a visual exploration of the act of removal, celebrating the liberating potential that lies in the ability to erase and make space for fresh ideas and untapped creativity.

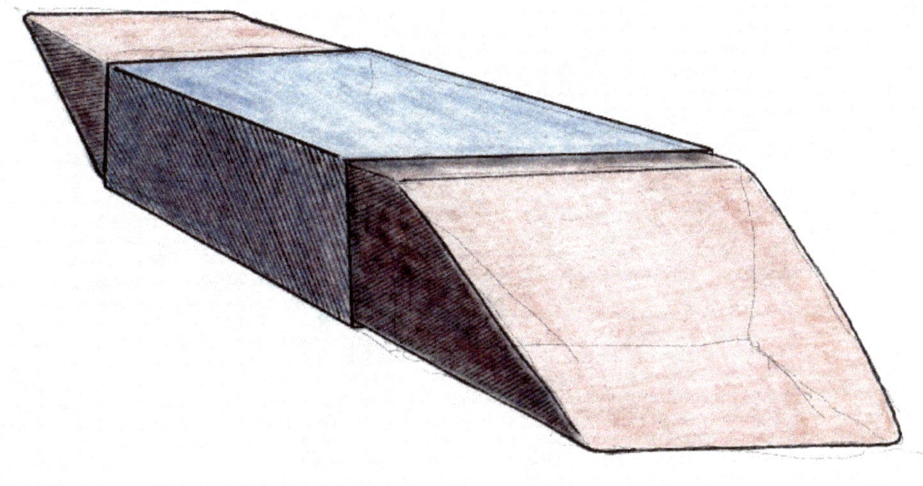

DAY XXVII
BEAST

On Day XXVII, the theme "BEAST" inspired the creation of a powerful and majestic sketch featuring a bear. The inked illustration conveyed the strength, resilience, and untamed nature of this magnificent beast. Each stroke sought to capture the bear's robust physique and untamed spirit, offering a glimpse into the wilderness where such creatures roam. Day XXVII unfolded as a visual tribute to the awe-inspiring presence of the bear, embodying the untamed beauty of the natural world and the wild essence of the theme "BEAST."

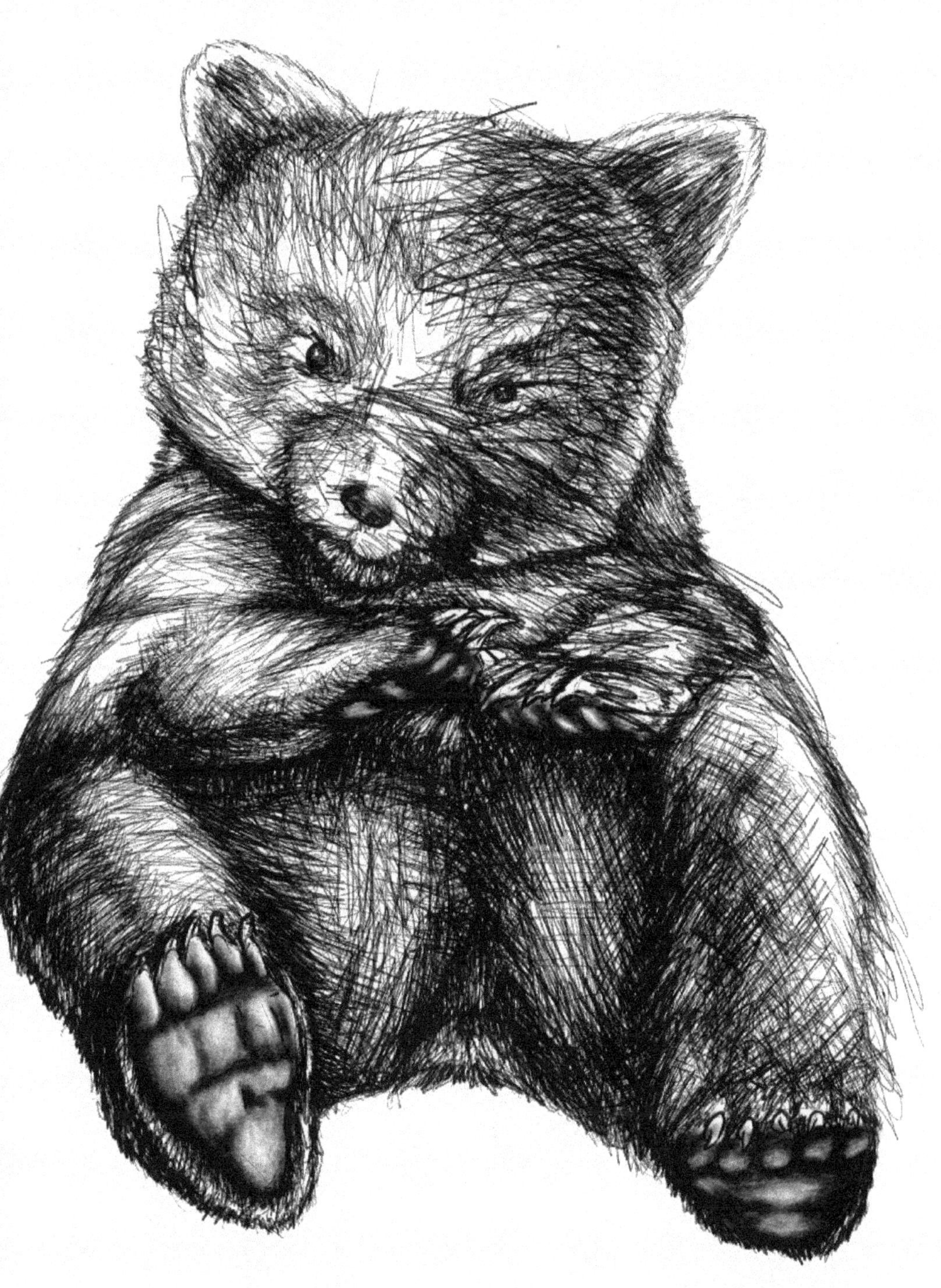

DAY XXVIII
SPARKLE

On Day XXVIII, the theme "SPARKLE" led my pen to craft a
dazzling sketch featuring a radiant diamond ring. The inked
illustration sought to capture the brilliance and sparkle of the
precious gem, with meticulous attention to its facets and
shimmering light reflections. The portrayal celebrated the
inherent beauty and allure of the diamond, symbolizing elegance
and luxury. Day XXVIII unfolded as a visual ode to the sparkle
that transcends mere illumination, embodying the inherent
charm and glamour encapsulated within the glimmering facets
of a diamond ring.

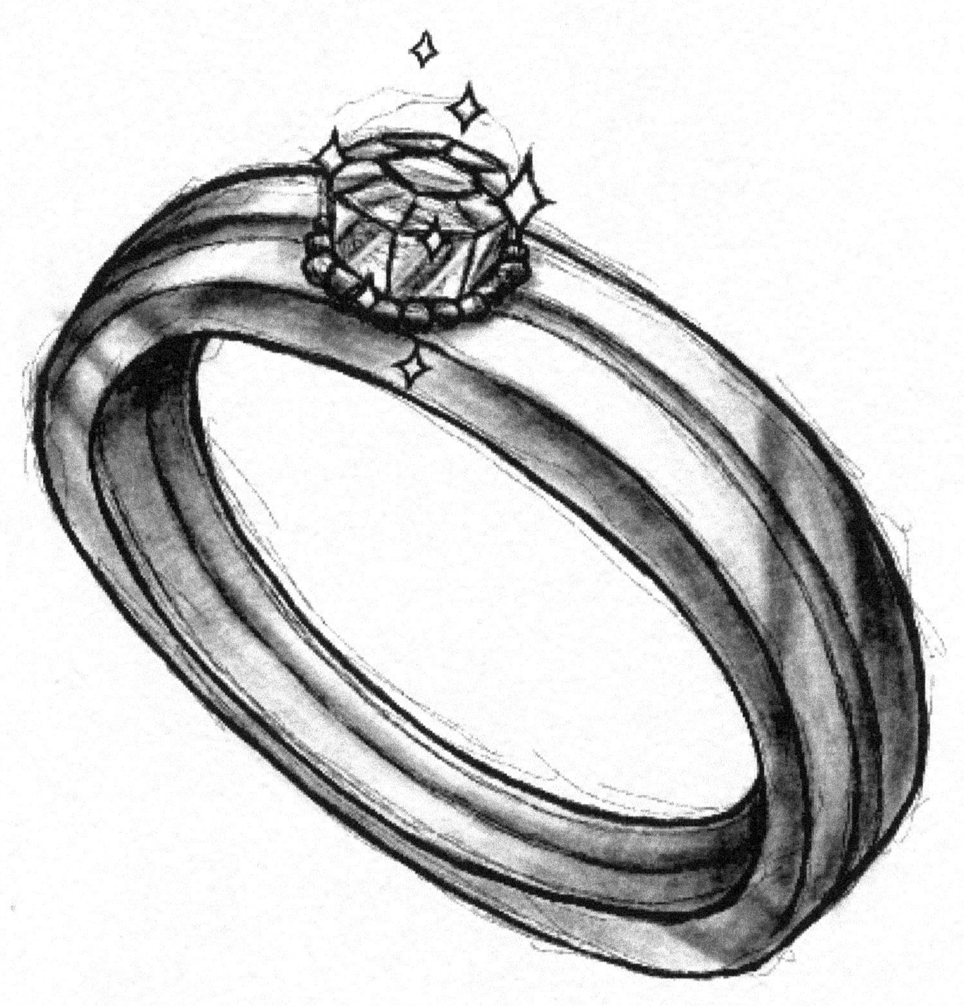

DAY XXIX
MASSIVE

On Day XXIX, the theme "MASSIVE" fueled my creative endeavor, leading me to embark on the ambitious sketch of a giant robot. However, the process took an unexpected turn, and the drawing assumed an oddly intriguing form. As I paused mid-drawing, the unfinished illustration became a whimsical reflection of the creative process itself—sometimes unpredictable, and occasionally taking unexpected and delightful turns. Day XXIX unfolded as a celebration of the massive and the unconventional, embodying the essence of artistic exploration and the willingness to embrace the quirks that arise during the journey of creation.

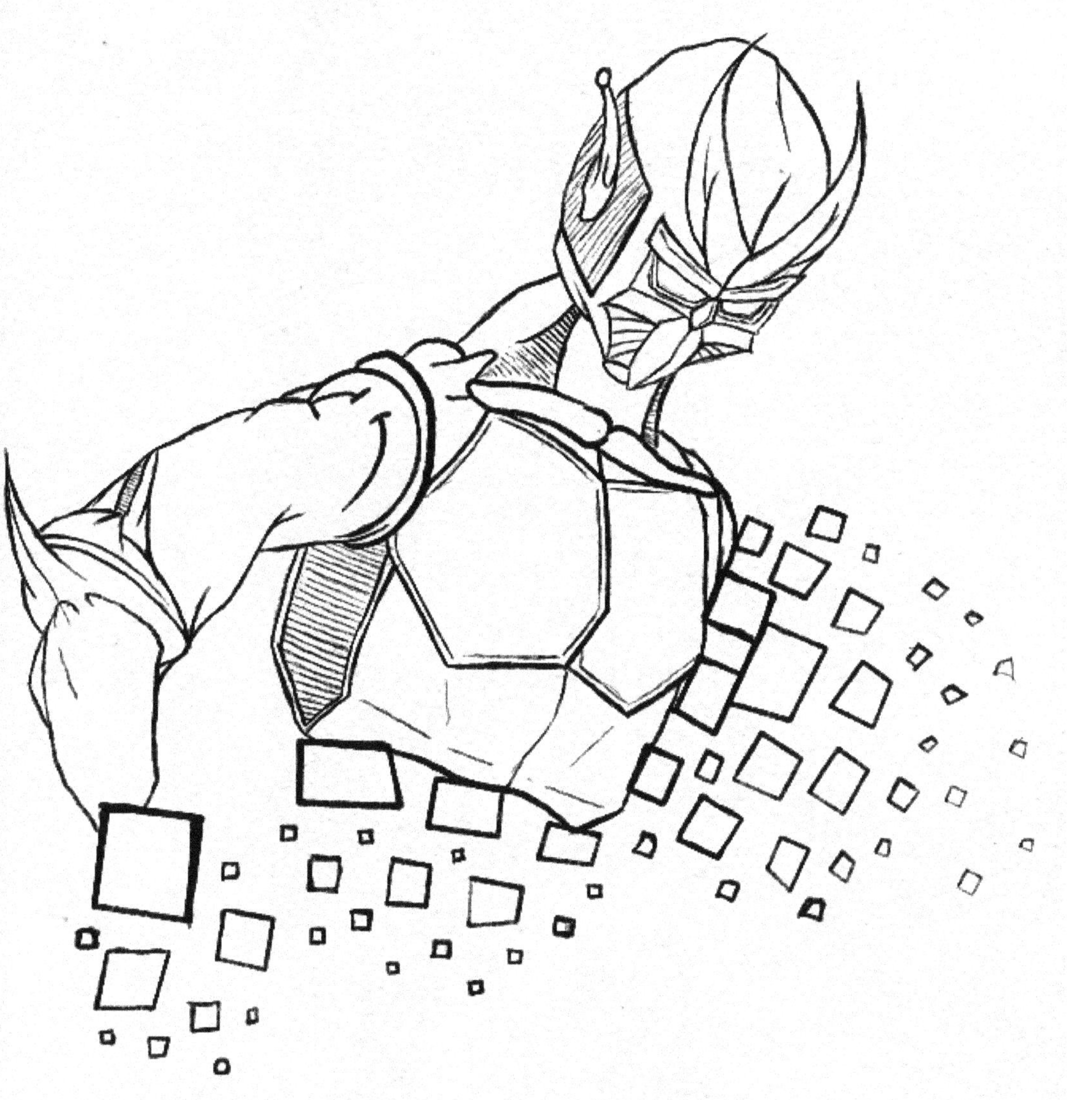

DAY XXX
RUSH

On Day XXX, the theme "RUSH" prompted the creation of a dynamic and exhilarating sketch featuring a speeding car. The inked illustration captured the essence of speed and urgency, depicting the car in motion with bold lines and a sense of forward momentum. The portrayal aimed to convey the thrilling sensation of a fast-paced journey, embodying the spirit of the word "RUSH." Day XXX unfolded as a visual celebration of movement and velocity, inviting viewers to experience the excitement and energy associated with the concept of rushing forward.

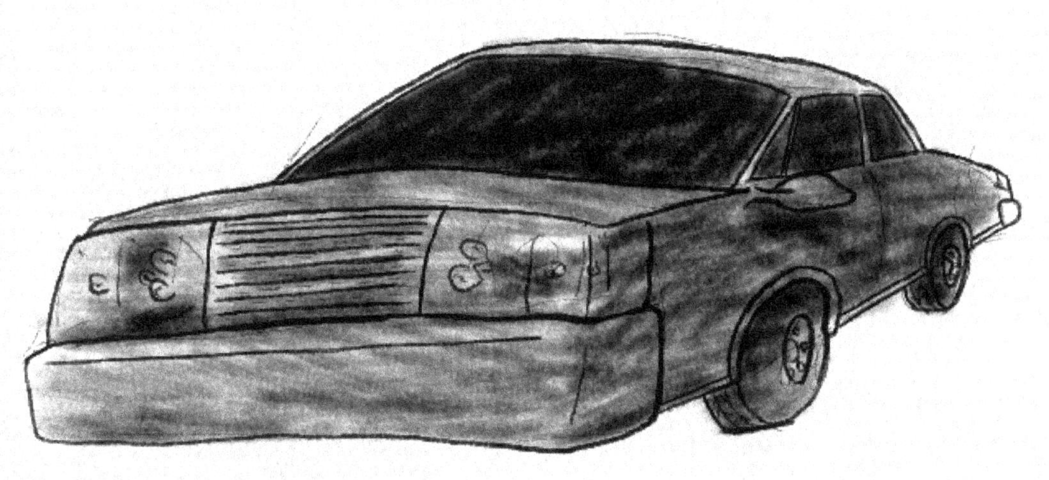

DAY XXXI
FIRE

On Day XXXI, the theme "FIRE" sparked a passionate and intense creation as I sketched a rose engulfed in flames. The inked illustration sought to capture the burning passion and fervor symbolized by the fiery embrace of the rose. Each stroke conveyed the heat, movement, and dynamic energy of the flames, transforming the delicate flower into a powerful and evocative image. Day XXXI unfolded as a visual exploration of the intense and transformative nature of passion, where the flames of creativity and emotion merge in a fiery dance, leaving an indelible mark on the canvas of expression.

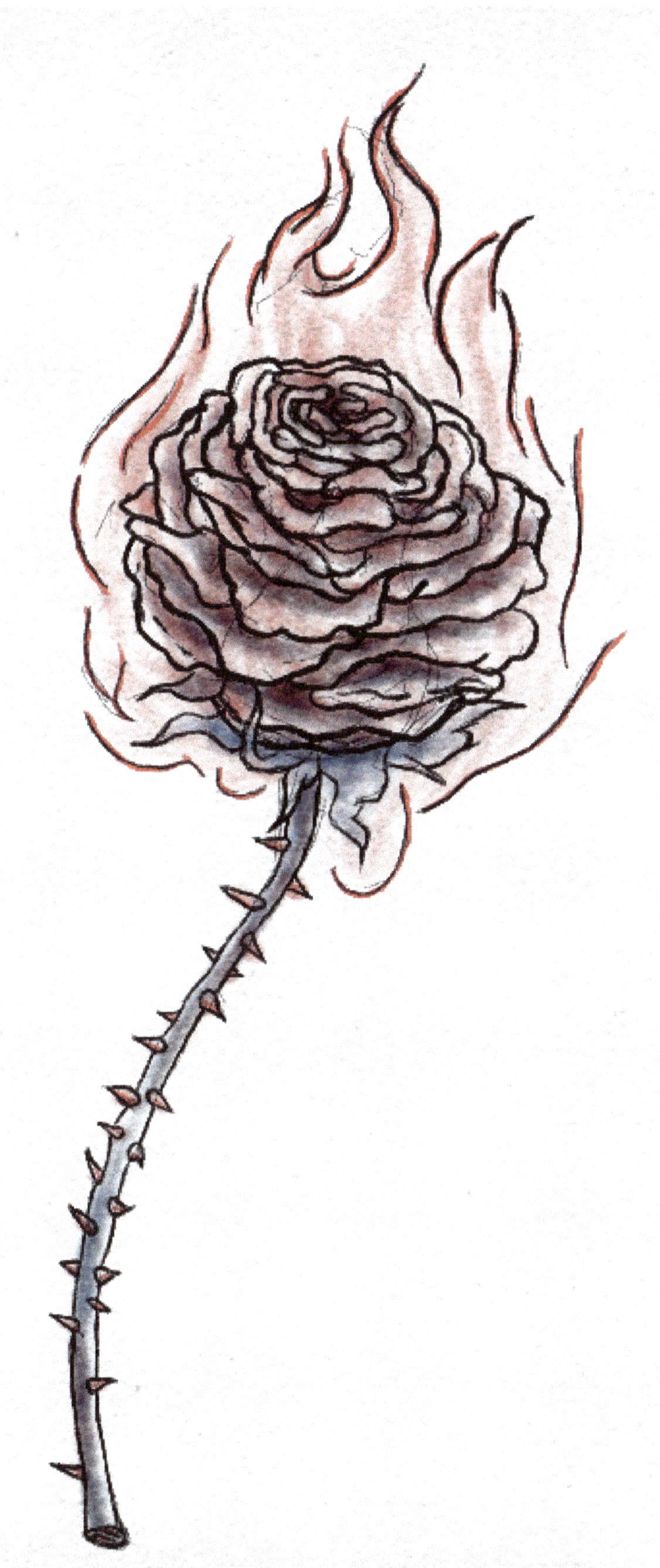

Epilogue: Inked Odyssey

As the final stroke marks the culmination of this inked odyssey, the pages bear witness to a tapestry woven with creativity, emotion, and exploration. Each day, themes unfolded like chapters, guiding the pen across the canvas of imagination. From the serene landscapes to the whimsical creatures, from cautionary tales to moments of unbridled passion, this artistic journey encapsulated a myriad of emotions and ideas.

The inked reflections of "ANGEL" and "DEMON" showcased the duality within, while "FROST" and "FIRE" whispered tales of the cold beauty of winter and the burning passion of the soul. "MASSIVE" embraced the unconventional, a nod to the unpredictable nature of creativity. Every drawing, whether completed or abandoned mid-sketch, contributed to the rich narrative of this inked odyssey.

As the final theme, "FIRE," engulfed a rose in passionate flames, it served as a metaphorical blaze of artistic fervor, leaving an indelible mark on the collection. The "Inked Odyssey" stands as a testament to the transformative power of art, capturing the ebb and flow of inspiration, the dance between light and shadow, and the beauty found within the imperfections.

May these inked pages be a source of inspiration for the reader's own creative journey, a reminder that every stroke, every theme, and every exploration adds depth to the canvas of expression. The journey may end, but the inked odyssey remains an eternal testament to the boundless possibilities that unfold when imagination meets paper and passion ignites the soul.

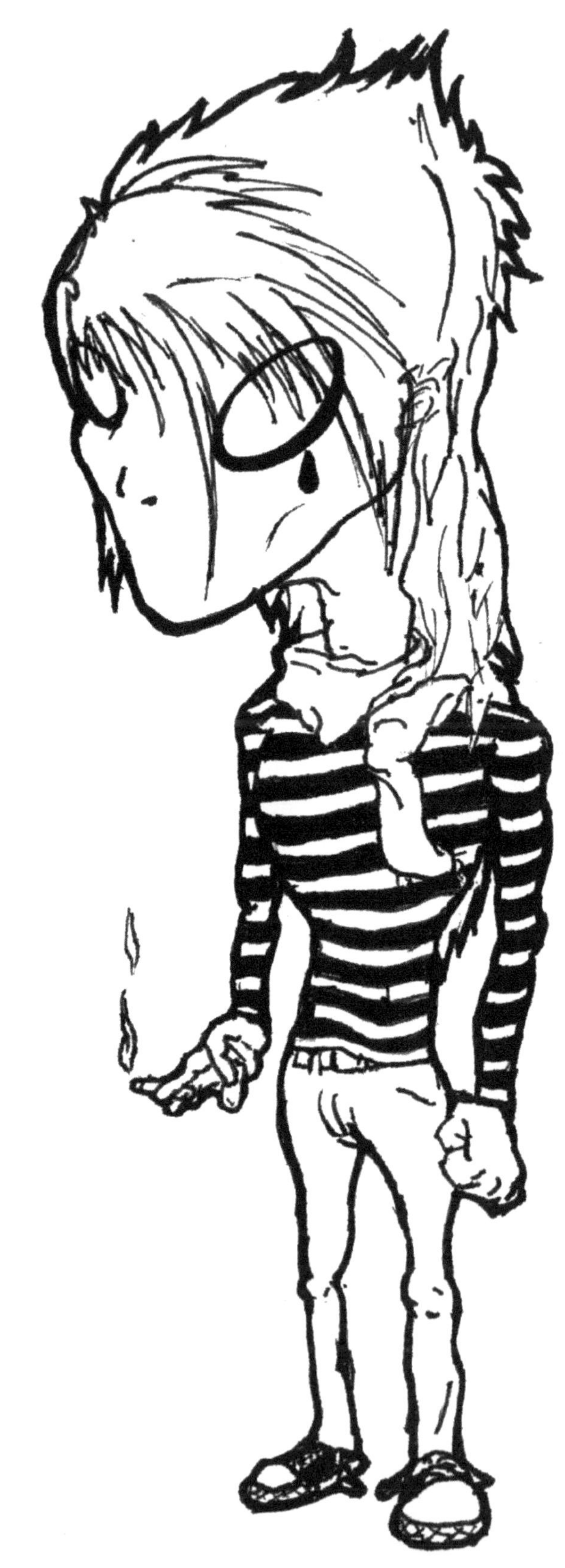

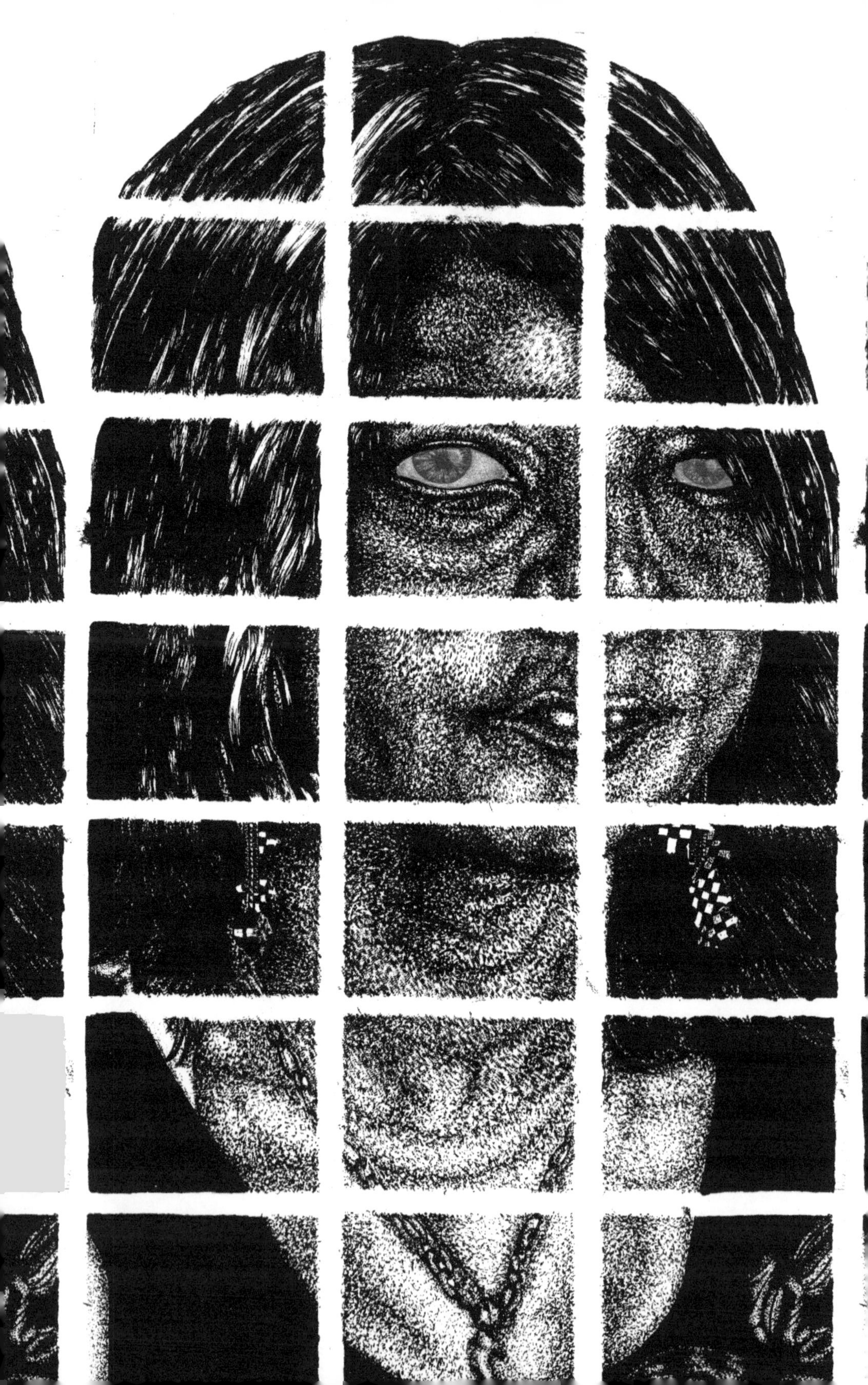

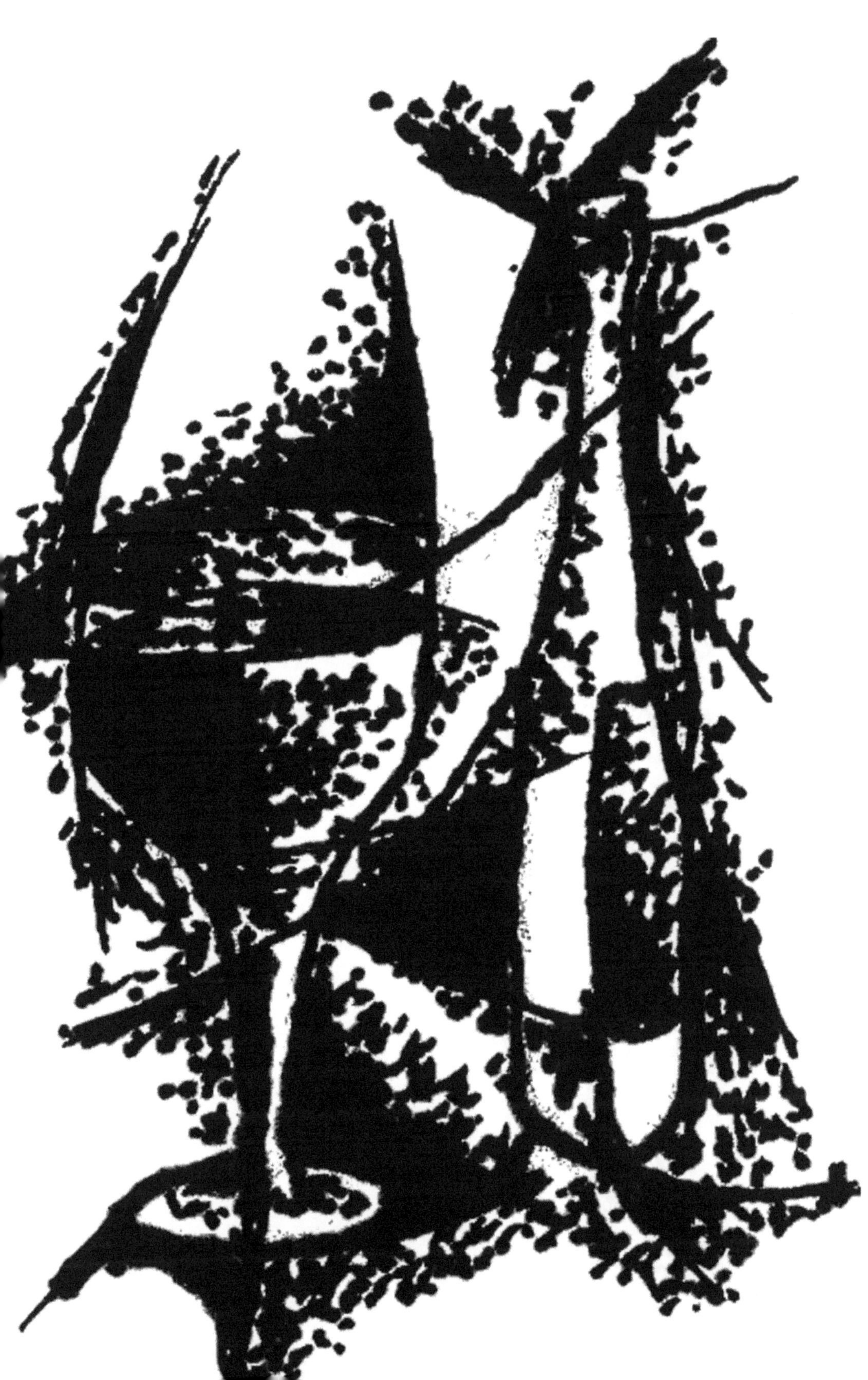

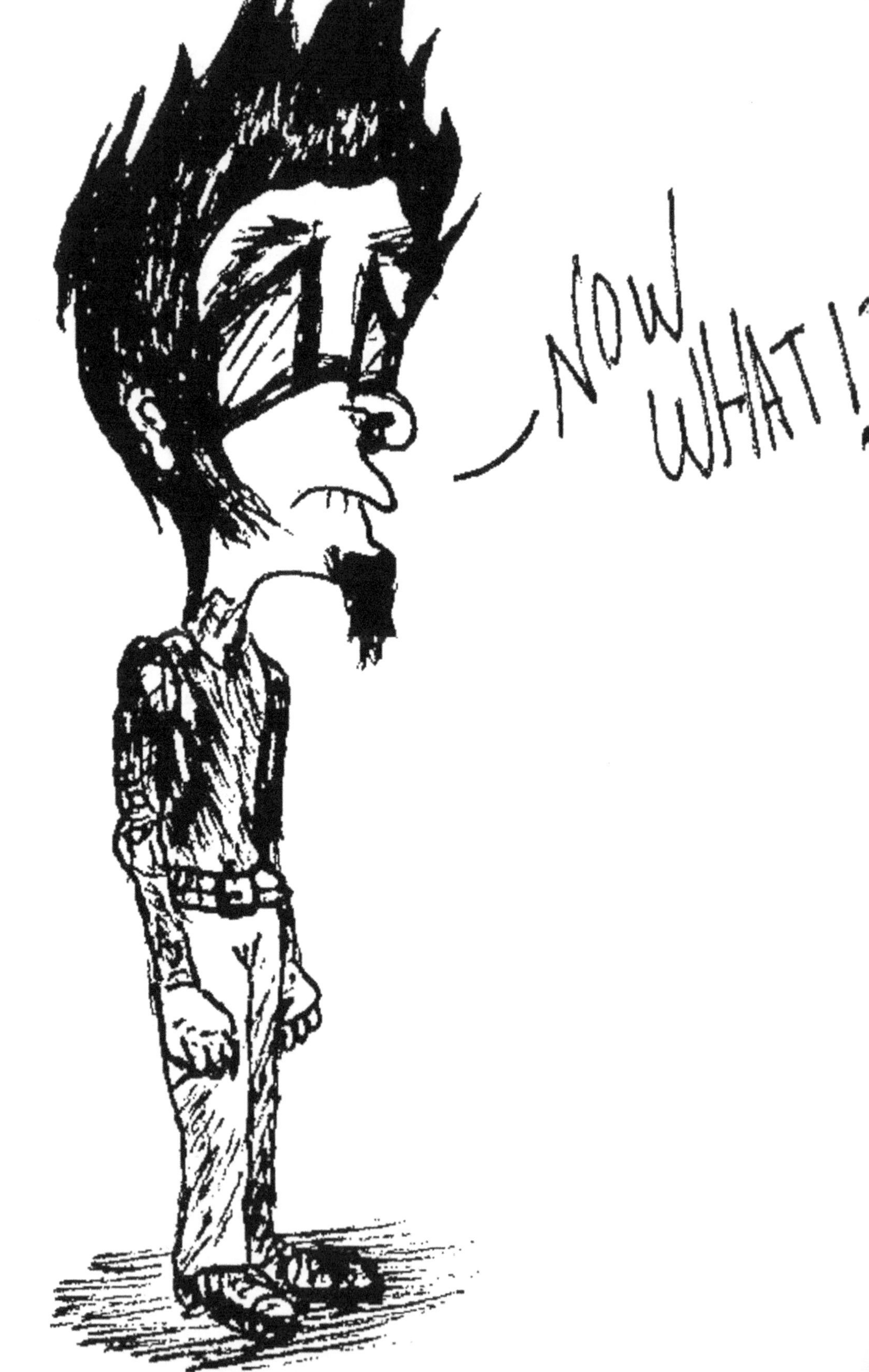
NOW WHAT!?

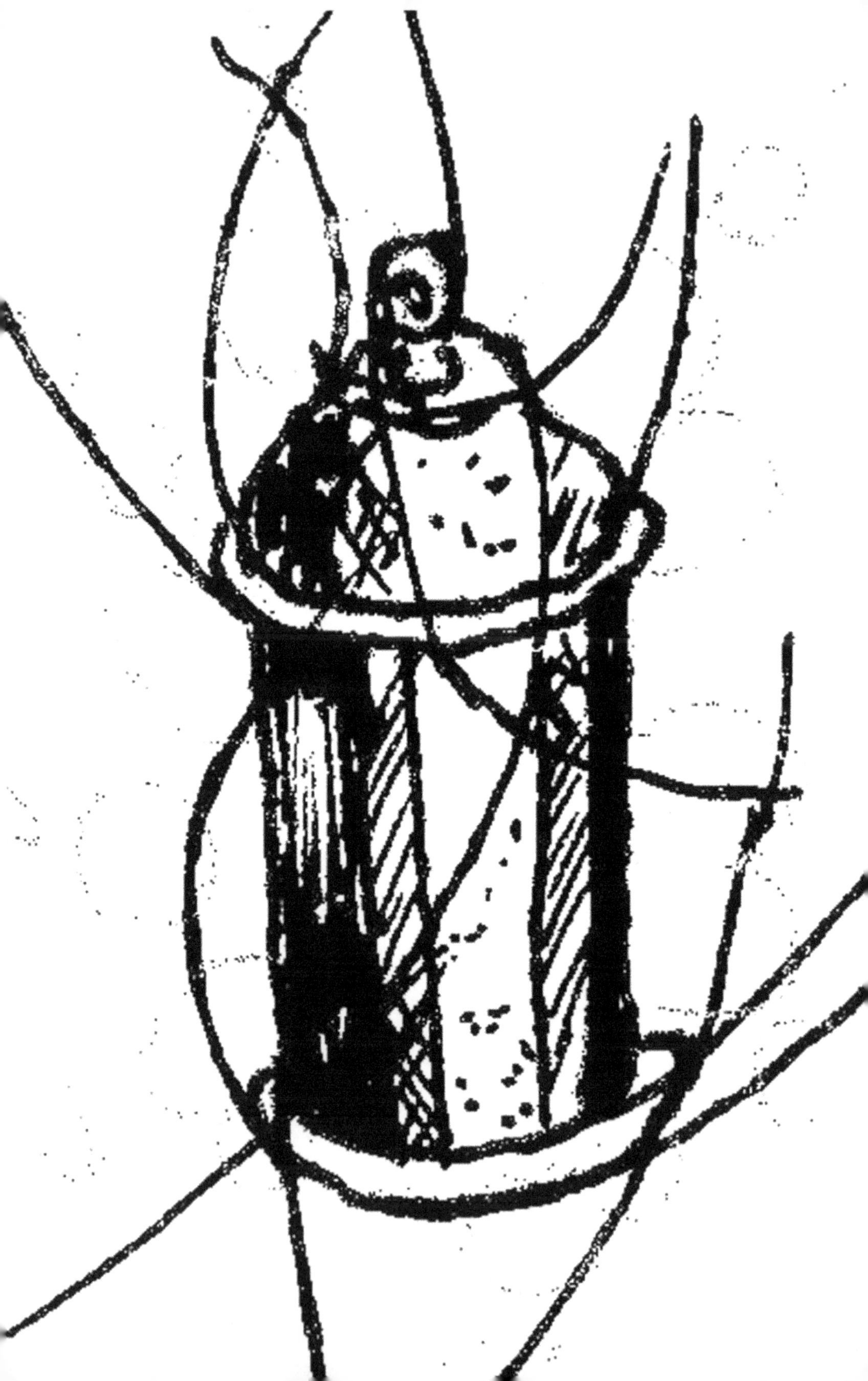

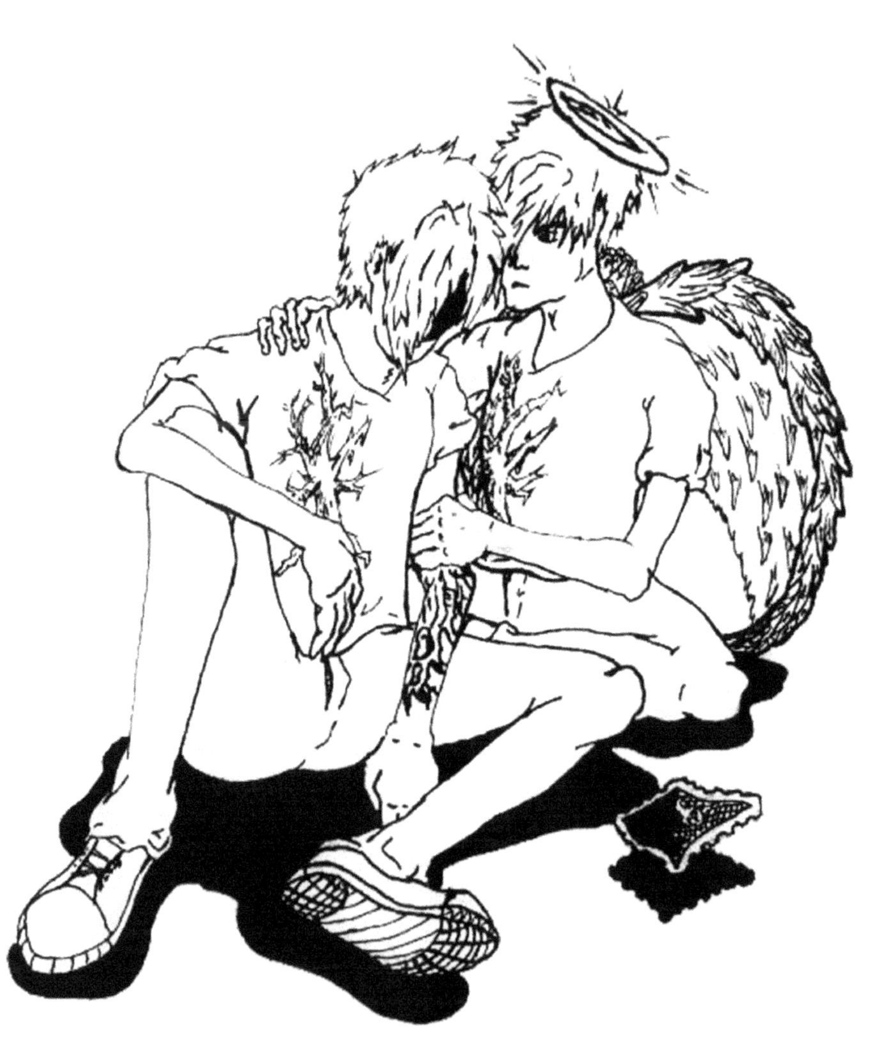